FROM REJECTION TO INTEGRATION
A Centenary of Service
by the Daughters of Charity
to Persons with a Mental Handicap

GW00506019

FROM REJECTION
TO
INTEGRATION

A Centenary of Service by the Daughters of Charity
to Persons with a Mental Handicap

Joseph Robins

GILL AND MACMILLAN

Published in Ireland by
Gill and Macmillan Ltd
Goldenbridge
Dublin 8
with associated companies in
Auckland, Budapest, Gaborone, Harare, Hong Kong,
Kampala, Kuala Lumpur, Lagos, London, Madras,
Manzini, Melbourne, Mexico City, Nairobi,
New York, Singapore, Sydney, Tokyo, Windhoek

Print origination by
Seton Music Graphics Ltd, Bantry, Co. Cork
Printed by Colour Books Ltd, Dublin

A catalogue record is available for this book
from the British Library.

This book is dedicated to the families
of persons with a mental handicap
and to all who work for them.

CONTENTS

FOREWORD

In 1884 the North Dublin Union established, in Cabra, a separate workhouse for children in order to remove them from the unhealthy atmosphere of the adult workhouses in which many of their parents lived. Eight years later, in 1892, when the Daughters of Charity took over the management of this institution they found a number of children with a mental handicap among the 400 residents there. These children were commonly regarded as 'idiots and imbeciles' and had frequently been abandoned by their families. There was little understanding of their situation or effort to meet their special needs.

Today the picture is very different. The Daughters of Charity Service for Persons with a Mental Handicap provides a comprehensive Service for 1500 children and adults which includes support and guidance for their families. The service operates in five centres in Dublin and one in Limerick as well as in a community living programme consisting of thirty-five houses in residential estates in various areas of Dublin and Limerick. Most of the developments that have taken place on a national level can be traced in this story of the Daughters of Charity Service.

The story throws into relief the vision, courage and love of the six pioneer Daughters of Charity and of their successors who included as time progressed an increasing number of lay colleagues. In their refusal to accept the status quo, they envisaged a better quality of life for persons with a mental handicap. In spite of enormous difficulties they worked steadily with the support of parents and families to bring about change.

However the most significant transformation which took place during the past hundred years was in the area of people's perception of persons with a mental handicap. The response of the adults and children to the opportunities offered them and the actualisation of their potential showed that persons with a mental handicap have both the right and the ability to contribute to society and to be integrated into it. This contribution takes many forms, not least of which is the enrichment of the personalities of those with whom they come in contact on a regular basis.

As the Daughters of Charity welcome a second centenary in the service of persons with a mental handicap they recognise the following goals and challenges:

- *To continue to provide a service characterised by love, respect, innovation and excellence, which strives to enable the individual to maximise his or her potential and to contribute to a society in which he or she is accepted and integrated.*
- *To work in a collaborative way to ensure that the rights of persons with a mental handicap, as citizens of our country, are respected and met.*
- *To recognise, in a world in which a person's value is often measured in materialistic and technological terms, that the person with a mental handicap has a particular role in 'humanising' society.*

In the words of the Service Mission Statement:

The Daughters of Charity Service for Persons with a Mental Handicap, 'urged on by the love of Christ' recognises that the person with a mental handicap possesses a unique dignity and potential, has a right to be enabled to take his or her place in society and in turn to contribute in a significant way to the enrichment of that society.

The Service is committed:
- *to the total development of persons;*
- *to working in partnership with the families of persons with a mental handicap, also with colleagues and other groups and agencies;*
- *to providing a service of excellence chatacterised by love, respect and creativity;*
- *to making a preferential option for people with the greatest need;*
- *to advocacy and to the promotion of justice for persons with a mental handicap.*

Foreword

In addition to the Daughters of Charity, the Service has many very dedicated and efficient men and women on its Board of Management and Central Management Team as well as colleagues throughout the Service. On them many of the future hopes depend.

Dr Joe Robins, in his book, meticulously documents the principal events in the history of the Service. His experience as a former Assistant Secretary of the Department of Health and his research on a number of areas of Irish social history make him the ideal person to research and present this story. All who wish to expand their understanding of services for persons with a mental handicap today are indebted to Dr Robins.

Sister Bernadette MacMahon DC
PROVINCIAL
Daughters of Charity
of St Vincent de Paul,
Irish Province

ACKNOWLEDGMENTS

I am grateful to the Sister Provincial of the Daughters of Charity, Sister Bernadette MacMahon, for inviting me to undertake this history, for her subsequent help in facilitating my access to information, and for her comments on a draft of the book. Dr John Cooney encouraged me to do the work, gave me a great deal of information arising from his own involvement in the service, and was a ready source of advice and comment during the preparation of the book. Sister Margaret Mary Altman identified the relevant archives at Dunardagh, and Sister Judith Greville helped me with the material available at Mill Hill, London. I had to turn to Sister Angela Magee for help and enlightenment on various occasions, and it was always given willingly.

To bring the human element into my story I depended heavily on the reminiscences of those who were themselves part of the story. I thank Sisters Louise Burke, Catherine O'Donnell, Mary Ryan, Josephine Flynn, Angela Magee, Rita Yore, Martha Hegarty, Patricia Lynch, Brendan Joyce, Gertrude O'Callaghan, Finbar Nagle, Marie Barry, Geraldine Henry, Catherine Tansey, and Zoe Killeen. They gave me a great deal of their time and helped me to create images of the past that I would not otherwise have found possible. So too did the residents, present and former, with whom I had conversations, particularly Bridie Fraughan, Annie O'Toole, Eileen (not her real name) in Glenmaroon, Agnes May, Chrissie Madden, Mary Roberts, Teresa Shine, Josie Hughes, and Nancy Quinn. I also had an interesting discussion with John Murphy, who spent about fifty years on the staff of St Vincent's, Navan Road.

Acknowledgments

Sister Gertrude O'Callaghan's typescript history of Glenmaroon provided me with information about the house and grounds there. Joe Fallon organised the processing of the book and was always available to help me. Other people associated with the Daughters' services who assisted in various ways were Sister Bernard McIvor and Pearl Buckley. Éamonn Ó Murchú of Scoil Chiaráin very generously allowed me access to his unpublished thesis on the development of special education in Ireland, and also let me have copies of documents that he had collected. Mícheál Ó Mórdha, formerly of the Department of Education, let me have his interesting recollections on the same subject, and Seán Mac Gleannáin, Chief Inspector in the Primary Education Branch, headed me in the right direction. Jack Darby, former Assistant Secretary of the Department of Health, talked to me about his memories of the development of the services. Pat Moloney of St Michael's House gave me the benefit of his wide knowledge of mental handicap in Ireland.

I am grateful too for the help of the staff of the National Archives, particularly Ken Hannigan and Una Warke; David Sheehy, archivist of the Dublin Archdiocesan Archives; and the staff of the National Library, Dublin. The typescript was prepared for me by Pauline O'Rourke, to whom I am very grateful, as I am for the assistance given by Catherine Killeen.

INTRODUCTION

Vincent de Paul founded his Congregation of Mission Priests — the Vincentians — in France in 1625. Wherever he worked in the French towns and countryside Vincent established 'Confraternities of Charity', groups of women of the district who bonded themselves together with simple rules to tend the sick and the poor. In 1629, as his work grew, he invited Louise de Marillac, a Parisian widow with high connections at the royal court, to help him manage his *charités*, a task willingly undertaken, for she was already noted for her charitable activities.

In 1633 Louise decided to devote her life exclusively to training country girls coming to Paris to care for the sick, and she founded a small community specifically for that purpose. This, in effect, was the beginning of the Daughters of Charity, although it was not until 1656 that the new order received the full sanction of the church and the crown.

In directing the manner in which the new community should undertake its work, Vincent ordained that the sisters be uncloistered and that they go about their activities unrestricted by rigid rules so that they could always be available where the need was greatest. In accordance with their vows they bound themselves 'to the service — bodily and spiritual — of the poor and the sick — our masters.' In the course of giving that service they came to Ireland in 1855 at the invitation of Archbishop Joseph Dixon, Primate of All Ireland, and established their first house at Drogheda. Two years later they founded two houses on the northern side of the city of Dublin, one in North William Street, where they opened a school and an orphanage for girls, and the other in Fairview, where they established a mental hospital for women. Here, working in districts where there was large-scale poverty and many overcrowded tenements, they soon came to the notice of the guardians of the North Dublin Union, the poor law authority responsible for dispensing public charity in the area. In time an association with the workhouse of the North Dublin Union would lead to the development of a service specifically for people with mental handicap, which would grow into a remarkable realisation of the ideals set by Vincent de Paul over three hundred years ago.

THE BEGINNINGS

OF THE

CABRA AUXILIARY

Towards the end of 1892 the Daughters of Charity accepted responsibility for the running of what was known as the Cabra Auxiliary, a workhouse school operated by the poor law guardians for the North Dublin Union. It marked the beginning of the Daughters' connection with an institution that would later become St Vincent's Home, the main centre of their work for people with mental handicap in Ireland.

To understand fully the nature of the task accepted by the Daughters in 1892 it will help to be aware of the poor law machinery of the period, the philosophy underlying it, and the circumstances that gave rise to the establishment of the school.

By an enactment of 1838 a poor law system was established as a response to the rapidly deteriorating social conditions in Ireland. The population had increased to over eight million and was continuing to expand; there was little employment; the quality of life for the masses was barely above subsistence level at the best of times; there were regular famines and epidemics; and there was considerable popular agitation. The main element in the new provisions was a national network of 130 workhouses — or 'poorhouses', as they became known — administered by local boards of guardians elected by property owners and financed by a local property tax or 'rate'. The purpose of the workhouse was to relieve destitution, and at first there was no outdoor relief in money or kind. A starving person had a simple choice: die by the roadside or enter the workhouse. A destitute family had the same choice. If they opted for

1

the workhouse the whole family had to enter together, and the parents and children were separated and sent to different units. Later in the century, when limited outdoor relief was conceded, it was used only as an exceptional measure, and the pressure on most of those seeking help continued to be on admission to the workhouse.

The environment and regimen of the workhouses were harsh in the extreme. They were built quickly in the early 1840s and, while durable in design, were of the cheapest and most spartan description. All decoration and notions of comfort were deliberately excluded, for the buildings were meant to be forbidding and punitive. This was emphasised by high surrounding walls, the breaking up of the family unit on admission, the workhouse garb, with the name of the union emblazoned prominently on it, the sparse meals, and the harsh regimen, which included imprisonment in the local jail when certain rules were broken. Everything about the organisation and operation of the workhouse was aimed at ensuring that none of its inmates found any inclination to prolong their stay there and that they developed what the Poor Law Commissioners referred to as 'a wholesome desire to go elsewhere.'

Although there was an amelioration of the poor law and of workhouse conditions during the later decades of the nineteenth century, the system remained based on a harsh, deterring approach, largely motivated by a policy of protecting the reluctant ratepayers from the excessive cost of poverty.

Yet despite the repellent features of the system, huge numbers of the Irish population were driven to seek refuge in the workhouses, particularly during the Great Famine and immediate post-Famine years. Although there were improving social conditions during the later years of the century, poverty remained high, the usual daily population of the workhouses being around 50,000 people, including from 6,000 to 9,000 children.

By the 1890s the population of the workhouses had taken on certain characteristics. It included an element for whom the system had been primarily intended: those who were destitute because of temporary misfortune and whose stay would normally be a brief one. The other residents represented a range of human misfortune and deprivation for whom the workhouse offered the only haven and who were likely to remain long-term residents. They included itinerant beggars who moved from workhouse to workhouse; a delinquent element, including prostitutes and young criminals, often the produce of an earlier workhouse upbringing; a large group of infirm old people no longer able to care for themselves; so-called idiots and imbeciles, mentally handicapped people for whom there was as yet no special public provision; lunatics unable to secure admission to the overcrowded district lunatic asylums; unmarried mothers and their so-called illegitimate children; rejects of a disapproving society; and orphaned and abandoned children.

Within this gallimaufry of human misery there was no more pitiable nor vulnerable group than the children whose circumstances had condemned them to a poorhouse upbringing. This background stigmatised them in the outside world, where they were universally regarded as bastards or 'workhouse gets' (even though many of them were in fact children of married parents). Apart from any other disadvantages it might have imposed on the children, there was widespread evidence that life in the workhouse led to a demoralisation of those who grew up within its walls. Official reports on the prisons and reformatories from the 1860s onwards reflect the extent to which children reared in the workhouse setting became delinquent. Describing the young criminals of the reformatories in 1863, a government inspector wrote, 'many of the children had known but two homes — the poorhouse and the gaol.'

The central authorities responsible for overseeing the workhouses — the Irish Poor Law Commissioners and their successor from 1872, the Local Government Board for Ireland — were, for a considerable period, reluctant to concede the unsuitability of the workhouse for children. Nevertheless there were important developments that showed a growing appreciation of the needs of children in care. A boarding-out system introduced in 1862 permitted the placing of orphaned and destitute children with foster-parents, but for many years this was applied only on a very limited scale by local boards of guardians who saw it as an extension of outdoor relief, to which they were opposed. After 1850, largely under the influence of Archbishop (later Cardinal) Cullen, who was distrustful both of Protestant missionary organisations and of the workhouse system, there was a considerable provision of Catholic orphanages under the control of religious organisations, including the Daughters of Charity.

A further development was the establishment by legislation in 1868 of industrial schools for certain classes of children under fourteen years of age who were considered to be exposed to crime. They included children found begging or wandering about without a home.

The effect of the various special provisions for children was to bring about a considerable reduction in the child population of the workhouses. By 1899 there were about 8,400 young children in seventy-one industrial schools operated mainly by religious orders, compared with about 6,000 children in the workhouses, many of whom would have been accompanied by their parents.

NORTH DUBLIN UNION WORKHOUSE

Measured by the size of the pauper population for which it was responsible, the North Dublin Union was one of the biggest in the country. It covered an area with considerable poverty, particularly in the densely crowded tenements of the inner city. In addition, its workhouse had to deal with a large vagrant population of rural origin who traditionally sought shelter in the former Dublin House of Industry, a complex of buildings that had been located on the site of the existing workhouse. When the North Dublin Union was formed, some of the buildings already there were designated a workhouse, and the associated hospitals (the Richmond, Whitworth, and Hardwicke) continued in existence but independently of the workhouse.

During 1889 the average daily population of the workhouse was 2,680, including hundreds of children, and the inmates were, on average, spending sixty-one days there, an indication that there was a preponderance of long-term residents.

From the beginning of the workhouse system the government had rejected any notion that workhouse children might attend daily at the local national school. Education within the workhouse was seen as an integral element of a policy that regarded it as essential that recipients of public charity, adults and children, be made conscious of their diminished social status. In any event the parents of ordinary national-school children would have been opposed to what they saw as the contaminating influence of the children of the workhouse. Yet, given the nature of their inmates, the government realised that the moral environment of the large city workhouses in particular was a most unsuitable one for young children.

A commission looking at the general operation of the workhouses in 1879 expressed the view that schools within the walls of the North and South Dublin Unions 'must be unavoidably exposed to much deteriorating influences. The first object in these areas is to keep the children in establishments wholly separated from but within reasonable distance of the workhouse.' The commission considered that with separate workhouse schools in the city areas and with improved administration in the schools of rural unions 'there is no reason why the education of pauper children in Ireland should not be as satisfactorily provided for . . . as any other system of education in any other part of the kingdom.'

By this time the guardians of the North Dublin Union workhouse had already moved some of the children away from the main premises in North Brunswick Street. The boys were housed in an auxiliary workhouse in Glasnevin called the 'Sheds', where they were trained in growing vegetables on land attached to it. They were marched daily to the main workhouse, where they had classes and where some of them also received training in shoemaking and carpentry. The workhouse girls continued to live in the main building, where they were taught laundering, knitting, and needlework. The boys given training in growing vegetables appeared to do it well. They were awarded prizes when on one occasion they entered some of their produce for an RDS horticultural show at Ballsbridge — but the prizes were subsequently withheld when private growers objected to the notion that pauper children, dependent on public funds for their maintenance, should be handed prizes for their efforts.

The 'Sheds', as the name suggests, were purely temporary premises and were, in any event, not large enough to allow all the children to be moved outside the main workhouse walls. During 1884 the vice-president of the Local Government Board for Ireland, Henry Robinson, informed a government commission looking into the operation of the reformatories and industrial schools that the North Dublin Union had decided to establish a separate school that would be an agricultural school for boys. He said that, as many of the deserted and orphan children in the workhouse had been placed with foster-families, the school would be primarily for boys who had parents in the workhouse.

The new school was opened towards the end of 1884 at Cabra, close to the walls of the Phoenix Park, on twenty acres of land. It was located in a quiet rural environment; it would be some time before it would be embraced by the expanding suburbs of the city. Built in the austere style of a typical poor law institution, it became known as the Cabra Auxiliary Workhouse, and, despite the original intentions, accommodated both boys and girls who had been transferred with a number of pauper assistants and teachers from the main workhouse.

In October 1888 the Guardians decided to employ six Dominican nuns, who had a convent close by, to teach and care for the girls. While the guardians had succeeded in geographically distancing the children from the main workhouse, the preponderance of pauper staff within the new building and the insistence on a workhouse regimen meant that the poorhouse atmosphere and influences were still present. It was not a setting that appealed to the Dominican nuns, and in early 1892 they told the guardians that they were anxious to terminate their work in the school. They were, in any event, primarily teachers, whose main commitment at the time was to the advancement of a school for the deaf that they were developing locally.

INVOLVEMENT OF DAUGHTERS OF CHARITY

It was in these circumstances that the workhouse guardians turned their attention to the possibility that the Daughters of Charity might be induced to take over the care of the children. The guardians were already familiar with the capabilities of the Daughters, since some of them had been working in the main workhouse and the hospitals of the union since 1888. Up to then the staff of the North Dublin Union had, like other workhouses, consisted to a great extent of poorly paid assistants drawn from long-term inmates who were happy enough to accept the token wages and the additional food and other minor concessions that went with their new status. The 'nurses' who looked after the sick and the infirm in the workhouse wards were predominantly unmarried mothers, untrained in every way, often with neither the disposition nor the aptitude for the work but selected for it because, as outcasts, they were relatively long-term residents of the workhouse.

From the 1880s onwards some boards of guardians, including the North Dublin Union, seeking to improve the care of their sick inmates, began to reduce their dependence on pauper nurses.

They were impressed by the discipline and caring qualities of the religious orders and attracted by their preparedness to work for little reward. 'They come very cheap here,' wrote the clerk of the Wexford Guardians in 1886, tipping off another board to the fact that nuns were prepared to work for a mere £20 or £30 a year.

The North Dublin Union guardians had begun to search for nuns for their workhouses as early as 1884, and eventually approached the Daughters of Charity. The Daughters had special attractions. They were not a convent-bound community: they saw their mission as working freely among all wretched and disadvantaged groups of society who might benefit from their care. Some of them were already deeply involved with the poor in parts of the city area served by the North Dublin Union. They had a particular interest in homeless children, and were operating an orphanage in North William Street. All in all, their experience and commitment would add greatly to the care of the sick and infirm inmates in the workhouse infirmaries.

But it is clear from the records of the period that there were also certain religious and political undercurrents at work with regard to the participation of the Daughters in the services of the North Dublin Union. From the 1850s onwards the affairs of the North Dublin workhouse had flared up periodically into religious controversy. Archbishop (later Cardinal) Cullen was at all times suspicious of the workhouse system in general and fearful that it would facilitate the activities of Protestant proselytisers. His suspicions were largely unjustified: the government went to great pains to prevent religious discrimination and missionary activities in the workhouses. Nevertheless the archbishop believed that they were being used for attempts to 'Protestantise' Catholic children.

If Catholic interests were suspicious of the workhouses, there were many Protestants who were concerned about the protection of those of their own faith in the workhouses, where the majority of the members of the boards of guardians were Catholics. The North Dublin Union in particular was viewed with some suspicion by the Protestant community. During the 1850s, as a result of Catholic inmates being encouraged to say the Rosary aloud, an anonymous satirical pamphlet, *The Pope in the Poorhouse*, was circulated in Dublin, claiming that such practices were tolerated because of instructions from 'the Castle' to keep the Catholics quiet by pretending to be liberal. Despite their majority on the board of guardians the Catholics themselves also remained distrustful. Dr Cullen's successor as Archbishop of Dublin, Dr William Walshe, maintained the attitude of his predecessor, and the records of the North Dublin Union show that he was a regular visitor to the workhouse, presumably to keep an eye on things.

When the Daughters of Charity agreed to work at the main workhouse and its associated hospitals in 1888 they had been encouraged to do so by Archbishop Walshe. He had asked them to provide eight sisters for the work, which they agreed to do. They were put under the direction of Sister Agnes Robinson, who was brought over from Liverpool for the purpose. It was, from the archbishop's point of view, a desirable development, as it introduced a Catholic influence into the institutions. From his own funds the archbishop gave the sisters money to meet the costs involved in taking on their new task, and discouraged them from looking for any reimbursement from the board of guardians, lest it should prove a barrier to the arrangement. Apart from any other consideration, Archbishop Walshe had inherited from Cardinal Cullen a distaste for accepting government funds that might in some way compromise the church on religious matters. The primary school operated by the Daughters at North William Street, for instance, had opted out of the national school system, as the cardinal and, subsequently, Archbishop Walshe wished the sisters to operate without a government grant and so be absolutely free with regard to religious instruction. This continued to be the position until 1897.

AGREEMENT TO CABRA PROPOSAL

When, in 1892, faced with the problems of the Cabra Auxiliary and anxious to improve the quality of care for its child inmates, the guardians again turned to the Daughters of Charity, the archbishop worked strongly behind the scenes to encourage them to extend their activities to Cabra. So too did the Catholic members of the guardians, who met privately as a caucus to discuss how the sisters might be induced to do so.

The first approach to the Daughters about going to Cabra was on the understanding that they would simply replace the six Dominican nuns and take charge of the girls. A favourable reaction from the

Daughters was quickly followed up by a letter from the chairman of the North Dublin Union, John Carolan, who extended the proposal and asked if they would also take charge of the boys up to ten years of age. All the existing lay teachers would be removed except one who would continue to teach the boys over that age. Under the new proposal no male staff would live in the premises except a wardmaster.

Throughout 1892 there were continuing discussions between the sisters and the guardians, both overtly and behind the scenes. Sister Catherine O'Grady, who appears to have been in charge of the sisters employed in the workhouse, acted as a reluctant inter- mediary between Sister Marcellus, Provincial of the Province of Great Britain and Ireland in Mill Hill, London, and the guardians. Negotiating with a public authority was an unfamiliar and uncomfortable role for her. She wrote plaintively to Sister Marcellus:

> *I would much rather these people would correspond to you themselves but they asked me to do so and I did not like to refuse.*

In August 1892 Sister Catherine wrote to her Provincial saying that the guardians were then pressing for the Daughters to take responsibility for all the children in the Cabra institution. Some of the guardians had approached her privately and had asked her to write to Sister Marcellus, hoping that she would insist on the Sisters going to Cabra. Sister Catherine wrote:

> *the guardians want everyone to know that the Sisters are to be the heads of the institution, acting, of course, under the guardians.*

The existing schoolmaster and schoolmistress would be retained for a period, since they had been there for some years and the guardians 'did not like to turn them away . . . later on it is sup- posed that these people will resign their posts.'

The proposal that the Daughters should take on responsibility for all the residents of the Cabra Auxiliary was not at first accept- able to Sister Marcellus. A Frenchwoman based in London, removed from the political and religious manoeuvrings of the Irish poor law system, she was opposed to her Dublin sisters taking on a commitment that, in her view, was beyond their resources. Writing to Archbishop Walshe on 22 August she said firmly that they would not take on the proposed extended responsibility because they had not enough sisters, but she held out the hope that this would be possible at some future date. For the present, however, she was prepared to agree only to the replacement of the six Dominican nuns then looking after the girls in Cabra. She also took the occasion to remind the archbishop of the financial consequences of this move. She wrote:

> We remember that in the case of the North Dublin Union Your Grace did not wish us to lay down the usual conditions on which the Community accepts works before the Board, as you thought difficulties would arise.

The Daughters, she pointed out, could not meet the expenses involved themselves as they did not receive dowries from their postulants and because each of their houses had its own charity to support.

It was left to Sister Catherine to communicate her Provincial's views to the guardians. Writing again to Sister Marcellus early in September she said:

> I told them what you said and I explained to them that you were only taking on what the nuns [the Dominicans] had. They seemed very much disappointed and they said they would have to see more about it and they would wait until Father Gavin came over.

Father Gavin, also based in Mill Hill, was the Father Director of the province, who was not only spiritual adviser to the Daughters but also chief mentor in relation to their business affairs. He came to Dublin almost immediately, and Sister Catherine later wrote to Sister Marcellus reporting on his meeting with the guardians. He was impressed by their determination to secure the services of the Daughters for the Cabra institution, and he saw no reason why the sisters should not take over 'the whole thing'. Sister Catherine herself was enthusiastic and bent on influencing her Provincial: 'It is a grand work, nothing but the real poor.' She thought that ten sisters would be required as well as a certified teacher for the school, as this would be a requirement of the National Board of Education.

Some days later Sister Catherine was again in contact with Sister Marcellus, saying that she had confronted the chairman of the board of guardians and told him 'plainly' about the financial needs of the sisters. She reminded him that the archbishop had met the cost of the Daughters coming to the workhouse in the first instance but added that they would not like to ask for his assistance again. Sister Catherine reported:

> *The Chairman said he knew it was a delicate point and that if it depended on the guardians you would have the money at once. It's the Government Board that will not allow this to be done. The Chairman told me to say that he would do his very best.*

It is clear from this discussion and from later correspondence that the guardians were having difficulty in persuading the Local Government Board about the merits of their proposed arrangements for the Cabra Auxiliary. While government policy at the period aimed in general at avoiding conflict with Catholic interests, there would have been considerable reservations about giving a religious community too much authority in a publicly funded non-denominational poor law institution. Later it would become commonplace, but in 1892 it was a new situation, and caused real anxiety to a Local Government Board determined not only to avoid religious controversy but to keep a tight hand on public expenditure. While eventually the board was prepared to agree to the Daughters being placed in charge of the Cabra Auxiliary, it appears to have been a reluctant agreement.

The Dominican nuns left the Cabra institution on 30 September 1892, and were replaced by six Daughters of Charity whose names had been approved by the board of guardians. Sister Martha Galvin, already employed as a nurse in one of the union's hospitals, was appointed matron of the institution with a salary of £30 per annum and given 'entire control' of it by the guardians, including charge of the teachers. One of the sisters was given the post of schoolmistress. The tradesmen who taught the older boys tailoring and shoemaking were transferred to the main workhouse, along with the boys who were undergoing instruction. There was some resistance to the changes by aggrieved displaced staff, and the chairman of the guardians felt obliged to write to the former schoolmistress warning her that his board would not permit any interference from the existing staff with the new matron.

Discussion on the more extended duties of the sisters and their management role went on over the following six months. The chairman of the board of guardians, John McDonnell, writing to Sister Marcellus in February 1893 said:

> *We are progressing slowly but I hope surely with Cabra; as we proceed the work appears to widen and develop a new feature in management every week. Those members of the board who feel a deep interest in the future of the institution are met at every step by sharp criticism and official [?] which I need hardly say heightens their difficulties very considerably.*

A fortnight later he wrote to the Matron, Sister Martha, detailing decisions that had been made on the outstanding issues. The lay teachers were being pensioned off, with the exception of a master who would be non-resident and responsible for teaching boys over ten. All pauper assistants would be taken back into the main workhouse, with the exception of a few who, if required, would be employed as farm hands. Then, resolving any doubts that existed regarding the management role of the Daughters, the chairman told Sister Martha that 'the full and complete management of the institution' was being placed in her hands.

Sister Martha was born Margaret Galvin in a farming family of ten children in Francfort, Co. Offaly. When she became a postulant in 1871 she was regarded by her religious superiors as somewhat slow, with little education or skills but of very willing disposition. She was probably a typical country girl of the period. Her personality and education developed under the severe tutelage of Sister Charlotte-Clementine de Virieu, the Frenchwoman who headed the Daughters of Charity when they arrived in Ireland in 1855 and who eventually came to Dublin to take charge of their North William Street house.

After her training Sister Martha was sent to England, where, before returning to work for the North Dublin Union, she was attached to a boys' orphanage in Enfield. She was a tall woman whose cold and rather severe manner concealed a kind and committed approach to those in her care. Her undoubted personal strengths were not always apparent to those only slightly acquainted with her. The chairman of the North Dublin Board of Guardians misjudged her. Remarkably, at the same time that he was placing the management of the Cabra institution in her hands, McDonnell was writing privately to the Provincial to say that he did not think Sister Martha was suitable for the post. In a carefully worded patronising letter to Sister Marcellus he wrote:

> *I am in candour bound to state that although Sister Galvin is most anxious to give every satisfaction to the board and is most devoted to the interests of the poor children confided to her care she is too gentle to hold her own against officials, rather timid in offering pressing and necessary suggestions to the board and not quite equal to the task of reconstruction and re-organisation that we have in mind . . . I assure you that nothing would have prompted me to write this note except a deep sense of duty, and fearing, by my inaction, the slightest shadow of failure might dim the brightness of your illustrious Order in this matter of management at Cabra. If Cabra is to be a success it will require a lady of wide experience, large heart, good administrative ability, who would hold a firm grasp on authority wielded, as I am sure it would be, by that admirable prudence combined with sound judgement that is one of the leading characteristics of your noble and self-sacrificing Order.*

McDonnell's *plámás* did nothing to unbalance Sister Marcellus's normal level-headed approach. She wrote to Sister Agnes Robinson, Sister Galvin's superior in Dublin, seeking a reaction to McDonnell's views and enquiring about her personal opinion. Replying in French, Sister Robinson left her Provincial in no doubt about her views: Sister Galvin had done a great deal of good already, the children in her care appeared very happy, and it would be a great pity to change her at this stage. It was Sister Robinson's view that, far from being too timid, Sister Galvin agitated *trop brusquement* with the guardians. She recommended that no action be taken; things would settle down after a short time. And so they did. Sister Martha Galvin proved stronger and more durable than McDonnell had judged her to be.

Thirty-two years later, in 1924, after a paralysing stroke that confined her to bed for the remaining five years of her life, Sister Martha retired from her post as matron of the Cabra Auxiliary after a life of devotion to the children in her care and, almost certainly, wiser in the ways of public officials and how to deal with them. Despite the fact that she had spent over thirty-five years in the public service, the Commissioners for the Dublin Union decided that she was not eligible for a pension. She died in January 1929.

LIFE IN THE
CHILDREN'S HOME,
CABRA, 1892–1926

The arrival of the Daughters of Charity in Cabra did not change the essential nature of the institution. It was a workhouse, and it remained subject to workhouse rules and regulations until the poor law system was abolished following the withdrawal of the British administration from Ireland in the early 1920s. While the Daughters brought to it qualities of care and commitment that were not there previously, the general regimen of the institution was based on workhouse principles. It continued to be designated an auxiliary workhouse in official records, although it was usually referred to publicly as the Children's Home, Cabra.

On average the population of the home came to about four hundred. Some were the children of long-term residents of the main workhouse in North Brunswick Street, often rootless vagrants. It was policy to separate older children from their parents, mainly to protect their moral welfare but also to deter the parents from remaining dependent on the workhouse. Infants and very young children were usually allowed to remain with them. Other children in Cabra were orphans or abandoned and unwanted, many of them so-called 'illegitimate children'. Some were physically disabled; others were mentally handicapped or, as they were then called, idiots and imbeciles, whose families had rejected them and sometimes abandoned them.

When the parents were known and were not destitute or themselves living in the workhouse, efforts were made to get them to contribute to the cost of their children's upkeep in Cabra. Collectors were employed for that purpose. Informers were encouraged and got payments from the board of guardians for giving information about the whereabouts of parents whose children were 'on the union'. In October 1895 a police sergeant who had successfully identified a woman who had deserted a male illegitimate child wrote to the guardians 'asking the usual reward,' and was given £2. The question whether he should not have done this piece of detection in the normal course of his duties was not raised. In January 1896 a man named Thomas Connolly told the guardians that he was in a position to give information that could lead to the arrest and conviction of parents of certain deserted children then in Cabra. The guardians decided to follow up the information.

The guardians maintained their supervision of the institution mainly through weekly reports from the matron, in which she was expected to refer to any developments or incidents of significance, particularly if there were financial consequences. There were also occasional visits from sub-committees of the guardians, who would meet in the 'nuns' parlour'. It is reasonable to assume that they drank tea on these occasions. Maintaining the quality of tea supplied to the union had always been a matter of importance to the guardians, who employed a tea expert, Mr Greene of Dawson Street, whose duty it was to taste the tea, usually purchased in quantities of fifty chests at a time. He obviously did his work well. A meeting of the guardians in December 1900 passed a resolution thanking Mr Greene for the competent manner in which he was performing his duties.

In addition to the visits from the guardians the home was subject to frequent examination by an inspector of schools on behalf of the Commissioners of National Education and by an inspector from the Local Government Board, who was responsible for monitoring the purely workhouse aspects of the institution. Their reports give some indication of the manner in which the home was conducted under the direction of the Daughters.

In January 1893, a few months after the sisters had taken over, the inspector of schools reported of the girls' school: 'General proficiency fairly good and the copy books are kept free from blots . . . Poorly prepared in grammar . . . Answering in geography was but middling.' He said that the girls made their own underclothing, assisted in making their own dresses, and knitted all the stockings worn by the children in the home. He found the general proficiency in the boys' school to be 'fairly good', although the amount of practical instruction was rather small, as there was no class higher than the fourth.

Later reports showed a progressive improvement in the schools. In January 1894, reporting on the schools in general, the inspector recorded:

> *The improvement in the appearance and demeanour of the pupils since the school was placed in charge of the nuns is very marked . . . A pleasing novelty in the instruction of the boys was the introduction of knitting; and in a short time so proficient did they become that the boys in third and higher classes can now knit their own stockings . . . A very manifest improvement has been effected in the reading . . . Copy books are wholly free from blots . . . The infant school is conducted with animation . . . musical drill . . . general proficiency is good.*

During the following year the inspector of schools continued to report favourably on the education standards in the home and on the degree of efficiency the Daughters had brought to the schools. During 1895 'singing was successfully introduced,' a new sound in the traditionally joyless workhouse.

The reports of the inspectors of the Local Government Board throughout the 1890s were also favourable. Despite the board's initial lack of enthusiasm for the new arrangements, it was quick to acknowledge the improvements that had taken place. In August 1893 the inspector reported:

> *There is a marked improvement in Cabra Auxiliary. The children look better and healthier . . . The whole institution has evidently benefited considerably by the increased attention given to it by the guardians who now visit it regularly.*

There were similar reports over the subsequent years.

As a result of the parsimonious approach of the government towards the financing of the workhouse system, the home was always poorly staffed, despite the dependent nature of most of its young inmates and the fact that at all times a proportion of them were physically or mentally disabled. With the passage of time, pressure for places in the home tended to increase. At the end of

1907 the top floor of one of its wings was partitioned, at a cost of £15, to accommodate sick children previously provided for in the main workhouse. Young children over two who up to then had been allowed to remain with their parents were also transferred there. To a large extent, room was found for the additional children by increasing the number being boarded out.

In 1910, when there were 214 boys and 173 girls resident in the home, the staff consisted of only fifteen sisters, one male teacher who taught the senior boys, a woman teacher with responsibility for the Protestant children, a night watchman, and a few paid assistants. Yet throughout the period of its management by the Daughters of Charity, no serious criticism was made of the efficiency of the home or its standards of care or cleanliness. An inspector from the Commissioners of National Education, reporting in September 1915, wrote:

> *The surroundings in which these children are living trained and instructed reflect great credit . . . Even without making allowance for many mentally defective children the efficiency on the whole is considerably above average.*

THE DAILY ROUTINE

The daily programme was dictated by workhouse regulations. It left little time for idleness. There was a standard regimen for workhouse children, which required them to rise at 6.00 and to spend several hours in religious and secular instruction after breakfast. Dinner, which usually consisted of bread, vegetables, and meat soup or milk, was at 2.00 and was followed by an afternoon of practical training or farm work. After supper at 5.30 there were more lessons, with perhaps half an hour for recreation, before bed time, which was at 7.00 p.m. in the winter months and 8.00 in the summer. Older boys and girls were often required to do tasks around the house and would have a longer day.

The sisters had little discretion with regard to the food given to the children. The diets and the amount and nature of the provisions supplied to the home were determined by the guardians, who in turn were subject to the dictates of lengthy regulations issued frequently by the Local Government Board. The matron, Sister Martha, tried hard to get away from the poor law strictures imposed on her, and achieved some improvements in the food and clothing, despite the periodic censure of the guardians. A contemporary of Sister Martha's wrote later that she had on one occasion threatened to withdraw the sisters from the home if the guardians went ahead with a proposed reduction in expenditure on food.

With the ending of the poor laws one of the first changes sought by the sisters in the enforced regimen of their institution was the freedom to feed the children in accordance with the recommendations of the medical officer of the home. This was sanctioned by the Minister for Local Government and Public Health in June 1924.

Now and then there were brighter occasions to break the normal institutional routine. Christmas was celebrated, but hardly in an extravagant manner. In December 1895 the finance committee of the guardians gave the matron £5 'for the purpose of purchasing toys and defraying the other expenses in connection with the usual Christmas fête.' Later the matron went through the convention of thanking the guardians 'on the part of the children' for enabling them to have a tea party and amusements on the occasion. Obviously it did not make all the children happy. The matron reported to the guardians that an invalid boy absconded during the festivities, after 'leaving the Chapel and saying he was sick,' and was later found to have rejoined his mother in the city.

By 1902 the matron had authority to spend £10 on Christmas fare for the children, and in that year the guardians added an additional £5. In October 1909 they provided two barrels of apples for the children on All Hallows' Eve. Shortly afterwards they allowed the matron £2 to take some of the children on an outing to Howth by tram; fares came to twenty-five shillings, and refreshments fifteen shillings. With the abolition of the poor law system the newly appointed Commissioners for the Dublin Union were a little more generous. In August 1924 all the children were taken on an excursion to Howth over a period of two days in two special trams, and 400 penny buns were bought for them.

An aspect of the regimen of workhouse children regarded as especially important by the guardians was their daily walk outside the workhouse grounds. It was the only contact they would have with the outside world until they ceased to be residents of the institution. But the purpose of the walk was not to keep the children in touch with life outside the walls but to advertise what the workhouse was doing for them. The Local Government Board went to pains to impress on boards of guardians how important it was that children be paraded publicly, clean and neat in appearance and orderly in behaviour, so that they would be seen 'by persons who would not otherwise have an opportunity for observing their creditable appearance, good conduct and suitability for self-maintaining employment hereafter.' As in other workhouses the daily walk became part of the routine of the Cabra home. The matron was required by the guardians to submit a weekly return of the number of children taken on the walks, the dates and times spent walking, and the names of the people in charge of each walk. Incongruously, the walking returns were accompanied by another required weekly return showing the gas meter reading, so that the guardians could keep a close watch on the amount of gas used in the home.

The long lines of children walking in twos, hand in hand, along the quiet, leafy roads and lanes of Cabra and the Phoenix Park became a common sight in the area. Almost certainly they looked strong and healthy, for the Daughters cared for them well, but there could be no doubting their institutional background. They were dressed uniformly in rough woollen clothes made in the workhouse, with the name of the North Dublin Union stamped prominently on them. This was not only to prevent the clothes being stolen but also to remind the children that they were recipients of public charity. When, shortly before the Cabra home was established, a newspaper suggested that this was a degrading practice, a Local Government Board inspector rejected the criticism as 'a little sentimental,' and claimed that workhouse children were 'not burdened with over-sensitiveness and are usually from that class that is deficient in the better feelings of self-respect and self-reliance.'

RELIGIOUS ISSUES

The fact that the children in Cabra were under the daily care of a Catholic religious order was a continuing worry to some members of the Protestant community who feared that the faith of Protestant children in the home was at risk. The guardians and the sisters went to great pains to avoid any suggestion of an attempt to influence the religious thinking of these children. There was, at all times, at least one Protestant teacher on the staff. The Protestant rector from Castleknock, who was chaplain to the home, kept a close eye on their welfare, visited them regularly, and gave them religious guidance. During the early years of the institution there was a small church for the Protestant children in the east wing, where they had sermons on a Sunday and were given instruction at other times. Later, when the number of Protestant children declined, the church ceased to be used as such and the children were paraded every Sunday to service in Castleknock parish church. When any of them became ill and required hospital care in the main workhouse they were kept separate from Catholic children there, at the request of the chaplain. In January 1896 he reported to the guardians that he had examined the Protestant children in the home in religious knowledge and found that they 'had been carefully taught the entire course of the Diocesan Calendar and knew it accurately and intelligently.'

The chaplain was, nevertheless, unhappy about the arrangements, and later that year the board of guardians included a provision of £300 for a Protestant church in the home when they borrowed £10,000, chiefly for improvements at the main workhouse. They had second thoughts about the church, and none of the borrowed money was spent on it. Later, in 1899, after representations from the Protestant Archbishop of Dublin, the guardians drew up plans for a combined church and classroom for the Protestant children, costing £900. The Local Government Board prevaricated, and following continued agitation by the Protestant chaplain and the Protestant members of the board of guardians a sworn public inquiry was held in April 1902 to determine whether the spending of public funds for such a small number of children was 'excusable'.

At the inquiry a Miss Pearse, who operated the Galway Protestant Home, offered to take the Protestant children from Cabra for a payment of £12 10s each per annum. A Catholic poor law guardian, Mrs Egan, who objected to the building of the church, supported the sending of the children to a Protestant home. She said that the atmosphere in Cabra was undoubtedly Catholic. She herself would not send a son or daughter to a Protestant school to be brought up among Protestants, and she claimed that, in any event, 'the children brought up in the workhouse were no good for anything.' But the Protestant chaplain, Canon Sadlier, was adamant about the need for a Protestant church in Cabra and would not agree to any alternative. The children, he argued, were entitled to their own place of worship like any other sect.

No action was taken following the inquiry. The Protestant members of the board of guardians remained unhappy about the religious welfare of the Protestant children, and in October 1902, when there were only eleven Protestant children in the home, a meeting of the board was held to consider the concerns being expressed. One Protestant guardian argued that 'a place where the atmosphere is Catholic . . . is not a place to bring up a poor Protestant child.' Another insisted emphatically that when Protestant children grew up in such an atmosphere 'they are neither fish nor flesh nor good red herring but are sort of milk and water individuals.'

The majority of the guardians felt that the views of their Protestant colleagues left them with no choice but to agree to the children being cared for elsewhere. Enquiries were made from Protestant children's homes in Galway and Kingstown (Dun Laoghaire) about the cost of maintaining children in them, but it is not possible to trace any subsequent action in the minute-books of the guardians. It seems likely, however, that the children were transferred elsewhere, as there appears to have been no further controversy about them.

The Protestant members of the guardians during the early years of the present century may have seen some threat to their interests in the attitudes and decisions of boards of guardians and other elected public bodies with Catholic majorities. Frequently discussions at meetings of guardians had little or nothing to do with the task for which they had been elected. A meeting of the North Dublin Union board of guardians in August 1902 spent some time congratulating Pope Leo XIII on attaining the twenty-fifth year of his pontificate, discussed recent enactments of the French government that they regarded as anti-Catholic, and voiced loud condemnation of a man named McDonnell from Chancery Street who had made 'unwarranted attacks' on the guardians. No other business was discussed. Another meeting concerned itself with the evils of landlordism and criticised the government for 'pandering to the frantic whine of Irish landlords.' A resolution was passed alleging that 'the landlord drones seek all the honey and the tenants and labourers take all the risk and bear all the toil.' On a later occasion, when some time was found to discuss the affairs of the Cabra home, it was resolved that all the children there should be taught their national language.

LEAVING THE HOME

When the children were between twelve and fourteen years of age the practice was to discharge them from the home as soon as employment could be found for them by the guardians. Invariably the work found was of a servile nature: domestic service and farm work and other tasks that required little skill and long working hours and offered poor prospects for their future. In February 1896 Kate Short, aged fourteen, was sent to work for a Mrs Doody in Chapelizod, who had a provisions shop and was prepared to pay the child £5 a year. Mrs Doody was said to be 'respectable and good'. Children leaving during 1900 usually entered employment that would give them £4 or £5 annually in addition to their keep. When an arrangement was made the children left the home provided with a new outfit of clothes, and the guardians and sisters ceased to have any further legal responsibility for them.

It was not always a happy parting, nor an easy entrance to a world where the children would now have to fend for themselves. They had been well cared for in Cabra but protected and isolated to the extent that many of them found it difficult to cope on their own. In addition they bore the stigma of the workhouse, a burden that meant they were shown little sympathy and got little support if they ran into trouble. A government commission of 1906 examining the operation of the poor law in Ireland was told that there were many children reared in Cabra who, after discharge, returned there time and time again when they lost their jobs or became ill. 'They look on it as their home,' said a witness. It was also stated in evidence that some of the boys on leaving Cabra developed into 'tramps', rootless vagrants, and that some of the girls, failing to adapt themselves to the life outside, had become residents of the main workhouse. Mrs Egan, the poor law guardian already referred to, alleged in regard to the boys reared in Cabra, 'that they are not in touch with the world outside; they know nothing of these places; they have only one line of thought — they are in the world but not of it. They are completely isolated from the outside world.'

And she compared the prospects of the Cabra boys unfavourably with those of boys who grew up in Artane Industrial School who later went on to 'gentlemen's places under good gardeners and ultimately became gardeners themselves.'

The unfavourable comparison with Artane was justified. That institution aimed to give a high level of industrial training to its boys to ensure their later employment, and it was staffed accordingly. The practical instruction given in Cabra was, by comparison, basic and far short of that required for a trade. In November 1910 the board of guardians acknowledged that trades were not being taught to the boys in Cabra, and decided to transfer instructors in shoemaking and tailoring there from the main workhouse. The guardians appeared happy enough that the house and laundry work and mending of clothing being done by the girls was sufficient preparation for employment. The girls were also receiving some instruction in poultry keeping. The sisters kept great numbers of hens, ducks, geese, and turkeys, and the records show that they caused dirty conditions in the grounds of the home, particularly in bad weather, and were the subject of occasional complaints from the guardians.

At this time the senior tailor in the main workhouse was William O'Brien, a prominent militant trade unionist. Before and during the years of the First World War he was involved in agitation about the wages and conditions in city clothing factories, branded by him as 'sweating dens', which would have numbered among their employees people trained in the workhouse.

Children fortunate enough to be boarded out from the home in their early years stood a far better chance of successful absorption into the life of the outside community. While there had been, at first, a lack of enthusiasm for boarding out, because it was feared that it would prove costly as well as appearing to admit shortcomings in workhouse rearing, it had become firm policy by the end of the century. Those to whom it was applied were usually lone children, the orphans, abandoned and rejected children who inevitably came into the care of the poor law union if they were not taken into the orphanages and industrial schools. By 1906 the commission reporting on the operation of the poor law had no doubts about the merits of the boarding-out system, including the fact that 'it was the cheapest mode of rearing children.'

Foster-parents, or 'nurses', as they were then usually called, were paid £7 a year for infants and £6 for older children, together with two suits of clothes worth £2. When the children reached thirteen years of age their nurses had the choice of adopting them or returning them to the home. There was then no system of legal adoption, so that adoption meant integrating them informally into the family with whom they had been boarded. This was done frequently. In November 1895 a relieving officer reported to a meeting of the guardians on three children with different nurses who had reached thirteen years of age and were therefore 'out of their time'. The nurses were willing to adopt them, and the guardians consented to the arrangement and granted the children the usual 'adoption suits'.

Throughout the records of the subsequent years there are similar references to children parting company with the home in this way. They were usually placed with families in the neighbourhood of Dublin, although the Local Government Board was not happy about workhouse children being boarded in or near the city and felt that their moral welfare could best be protected in a rural setting. Whenever the opportunity arose, children from Cabra were sent to country families. In 1905, for instance, eleven children were placed in Co. Wexford through arrangements made with the parish priest of Piercetown.

Sometimes boarding out ended in failure. In October 1895 'a girl of weak intellect and deformed' was returned by her nurse as soon as she was out of her time. In February the following year a number of children had to be taken from a nurse who 'had taken to drink.' Mostly, however, boarding out was successful; evidence was given to the commission already referred to that the children did not usually return to the home but were absorbed in the population. It was said that, in time, some of them became the support of their elderly foster-parents and that some married and 'became respectable men and women.' This was a happy outcome, and a considerable achievement given the social obstacles they had had to overcome.

BEGINNINGS OF
THE MENTAL
HANDICAP SERVICE

From its establishment, some of the children admitted to the Cabra home had been mentally handicapped or, as they were then called, idiots and imbeciles. Since these were unlikely to be placed in employment or to be acceptable as boarded-out children, their number accumulated and they formed an increasing proportion of the residents of the home. The problem of providing for them grew accordingly. By the early 1920s a practice that had developed of passing on handicapped children over fourteen years old to the Richmond (Grangegorman) Lunatic Asylum was being strongly resisted by the hospital authorities.

The problem of lack of provision for children with mental handicap was not, however, an exclusively Dublin one. It was a national problem, for there was no institution in the country providing specifically for them except Stewart's Hospital, a private institution intended primarily for Protestant children.

In other countries there had been for some time a developing awareness of the need for special public provision for mentally handicapped children. Most of the early work on the problem of mental retardation had been done in France, where basic ideas on special educational and training techniques were developed. As these ideas progressed, the first special institutions were established on the Continent and in Britain, particularly from the 1840s onwards. But the new concepts of care aroused little immediate interest in Ireland. In any event, even if there had been public demand for special provision it is unlikely that the government would have taken any action, as it had already created two extensive institutional systems, the workhouses and the district lunatic asylums, which between them were intended to provide for the whole spectrum of people requiring institutional care other than the sick in general hospitals. The rules governing the operation of asylums throughout the nineteenth century provided for the admission of so-called idiots and imbeciles, as well as insane people. As the asylums filled up, the workhouses took on a supporting role and accepted those unable to find a place in the asylum and who would otherwise be homeless or have no-one to care for them. By 1892 there were over two thousand idiots and imbeciles being poorly cared for in workhouses throughout the country.

The only special provision for people with mental handicap before the present century was for Protestant children. In 1869 a committee consisting largely of members of ascendancy families acquired a private asylum operated by Dr Henry Hutchinson Stewart in Lucan, Co. Dublin, and opened the Stewart Institution for Idiots, 'based on Protestant principles of the broadest and unsectarian character.' Later, when the Lucan premises became overcrowded, the management committee acquired the residence and demesne of Lord Donoughmore at Palmerstown, Co. Dublin, and early in 1879 transferred to it all the inmates of the Lucan institution. The new centre was named the Stewart Institution for Idiotic and Imbecile Children and Middle-Class Lunatic Asylum. In time the institution shortened its name to Stewart's Hospital and became wholly a centre for children and adults with a mental handicap. It would remain for almost fifty years the only special facility of that nature in Ireland.

Yet despite the dearth of provision for handicapped children during this period it cannot be said that there was any significant degree of agitation on their behalf. To a considerable extent mental deficiency was accepted fatalistically as a burden to be borne by families without any expectation of support from the state. When the children grew into adults those who could no longer be tolerated in their own homes were passed on to the workhouse or asylums, wherever they could be accommodated. Some of the more docile were permitted to wander abroad and, according to an official report, were 'often teased, often goaded to frenzy by thoughtless children, often the victims of ill-treatment . . .'

It was probably no worse a life than they would have had in the asylum or workhouse. They were often kept in 'cells' in the workhouses, small confined spaces with stone flooring and heavily bolted doors with small apertures near the ceiling for light and ventilation. A government commission commented in 1879 that the cells 'were more suited for the imprisonment of malefactors, than for the accommodation of idiot paupers.' Inmates considered 'harmless' were usually dispersed throughout the workhouse, where they shared accommodation with the general body of paupers. No special care was given, because they had been admitted primarily as paupers and because the workhouse was not organised or staffed to meet the special needs of any of its inmates. To the extent that they received any exceptional attention it was given by pauper assistants, who were recompensed for helping to clean and feed them by being given extra rations of tea, sugar, and bread. Needless to say, the assistants themselves were often of low intellect and dissolute background.

During the later years of the nineteenth century various government commissions, as well as the inspectors of lunacy in their annual reports, criticised the conditions in which people with a mental handicap were being kept both in the asylums and in the workhouses. The inspectors in their report for 1891 also drew attention to the fact that the great majority of such people remained outside institutions, 'hopeless wanderers exposed to want and suffering, residing in homes where they can only in rare instances obtain the treatment suitable to their condition while often they are grossly neglected.' As an example they quoted the case of a poor woman in Dublin who chained her imbecile child to a bed while she went to work every day to support the two of them. The inspectors urged the setting up of what they called a National Training School for Idiots and Imbeciles, funded by the government, because they were of the opinion that it was beyond the capacity of voluntary charity to cope with the problem. This recommendation fell on deaf ears.

During the early years of the present century it became official policy to move as many people with mental handicap as possible from the workhouses to the asylums. In 1904 over a thousand inmates, most of them mentally handicapped but including chronically insane, were transferred. In one instance only was special accommodation provided, when an industrial school in Youghal was designated an auxiliary asylum and over two hundred cases transferred to it from the workhouses in the Cork area. But there was a limit to the number that the already overcrowded asylums could accept. In 1905, after the transfers had taken place, there were still 3,165 people who were mentally handicapped or insane in the workhouses, some 'excitable and troublesome'. During the same year an insane person in Naas workhouse suddenly attacked five inmates in what was called the idiot ward and killed four of them — an extreme example of the vulnerability of docile people with mental handicap in the institutions of the period.

VIEWS OF GOVERNMENT COMMISSIONS

The years immediately before the First World War were marked by the reports of a number of government commissions that looked at, among other things, the problem of mental handicap in Ireland. A viceregal commission reporting on poor law reform in 1906 supported the policy of removing all mentally incapacitated people from the workhouses to the asylums or auxiliary asylums, but did not give it a high priority, believing that the sane sick had more urgent claims on the practical sympathy of the ratepayers. A more broadly based royal commission reporting in 1909 took a similar view.

Yet another commission, the Royal Commission on the Care and Control of the Feeble-Minded, reporting in 1908, contained the first comprehensive review of the needs of people with congenital mental defects both in Britain and Ireland. It proposed four classifications for them: idiots, imbeciles, feeble-minded, and moral imbeciles. It estimated that there were over 25,000 people in these classes in Ireland, of whom 7,580 were children, almost all of whom lacked provision of any sort. In its main recommendation the commission proposed that local authorities be statutorily obliged to make suitable provision for all mentally abnormal people, subject to the direction of a specially constituted central body.

Evidence given to these commissions provides us with information about the abysmal situation of people with a mental defect in the early part of the present century. Sir George O'Farrell, Inspector of Lunacy, told the Commission on the Feeble-Minded that their conditions in the workhouses were 'with few exceptions, deplorable.' Dr W. R. Dawson, medical superintendent of a private asylum, Farnham House, told the same commission that on a visit to the North Dublin Union he had noted that 565 of the inmates, about one-fifth of the total population, were mentally defective. Dr Conolly Norman of the Richmond Asylum, a strong advocate of special institutions for the training of people with mental handicap, described how in the asylums

> *old and young, low class idiots, high grade imbeciles, chronic dements and cases of senile decay are placed together promiscuously . . . The period of life when education might be possible passes away; bad habits are confirmed and become ineradicable.*

In the North Dublin Union workhouse people with mental handicap and sane people with epilepsy were herded together in overcrowded conditions; many of their beds were boxes filled with loose straw, for ease of changing in the case of dirty patients. In some of the asylums children who were handicapped were detained as dangerous lunatics on the basis of evidence that they had committed some trivial offence, such as throwing stones in the street. It was the only way in which a place could have been found for them. In 1909 one of the inspectors of lunacy, Dr E. M. Courtenay, noted child imbeciles scattered throughout the wards of the Richmond and Portrane Asylums.

One of the Irish witnesses appearing before the Commission on the Feeble-Minded was Sir Christopher Nixon, former president of the Royal College of Physicians in Ireland, who had been impressed by a colony for mentally defective people that he had seen in Ursberg in Bavaria operated by an order of Catholic nuns. He suggested that a similar colony would be ideal for Ireland and urged that one of the male or female religious orders be prevailed on to undertake the work. He mentioned a number of orders, including the 'French Sisters of Charity', whose work for the insane had impressed him.

But despite the various reports and the many recommendations, no action was taken. In Britain special statutory provisions were introduced in 1913. A *cri de cœur* from Conolly Norman summed up the situation in Ireland:

> *The greatest difficulty in doing anything for this class in Ireland is the common difficulty of focusing public attention on anything so little controversial as the care of the insane.*

There was, in any event, no demand for special institutions even from families where there was mental deficiency. Dr Dawson believed that Dublin parents of all classes were highly sensitive about any mental inferiority in their children; they would not be prepared to stigmatise them by sending them to special schools. Dawson, whose thinking was in advance of his times, advocated special classes in ordinary schools, with specially trained teachers. This, he believed, would be more acceptable to parents.

CABRA AS MENTAL HANDICAP CENTRE

Ireland was now entering on troubled and exciting times. The Great War started in 1914. Then came the insurrection of 1916, followed by the War of Independence and the departure of the British administration. The early 1920s were hard times, politically and economically.

Since the establishment of the Cabra home there were at all times children with mental handicap among its residents, and there are frequent references in the records both to adult and child handicapped in the main workhouse. In November 1910, for instance, the guardians asked Cabra to take four imbecile children from the workhouse, and passed a resolution regretting the lack of special provision for handicapped Catholic children. In September 1915 a school inspector referred to the 'many' mentally defective children in the home. But there were restrictions on the type of children the home could take. Its statutory role as part of the workhouse system was to provide only for children who were destitute; the fact that a child had a mental handicap did not necessarily place it in that category.

In 1924, when mentally defective children were being reluctantly admitted to the Richmond Mental Hospital (Grangegorman), the hospital's committee of management urged the Commissioners for the Dublin Union (a short-lived authority that replaced the poor law guardians for the North and South Dublin Unions) to join with them in seeking special accommodation for handicapped children then in the mental hospitals and workhouses. There were other demands for action, and the first important move came during that year when Archbishop Edward Byrne of Dublin asked the Daughters of Charity if they would be prepared to agree to operate the Cabra home as a centre exclusively for children with a mental handicap. There were at the time 54 mentally handicapped children in the home, among its total population of 502 children. The then very large number of residents arose to some extent from transfers following the closure of the neighbouring workhouse school in Pelletstown operated by the South Dublin Union, when the two Dublin unions amalgamated in 1918.

Apart from the archbishop's anxiety to secure quickly an institution that would care for some of the large number of Catholic children who were unprovided for, he had some concern about the fact that the Protestant-directed Stewart's Hospital was accepting Catholic children from time to time. From its early days it had been viewed suspiciously by the Catholic clergy. Cardinal Cullen had, unjustly, branded it a proselytising agency and given instructions that Catholics were not to patronise or encourage it, directly or indirectly. The institution was based initially on Protestant principles, it was unequivocally a Protestant institution intended primarily for Protestant children, and was not in any way involved in missionary activities. The form of application for the admission of a child at the turn of the century made clear its policy:

> *The benefit of the institution shall be open to idiotic and imbecile children of all religious denominations whose parents and guardians being fully informed as to its nature and management deliberately seek their admission . . . but the inculcation of religious principles being a necessary basis of the training of the children, the institution shall be conducted on Protestant principles of the broadest and most unsectarian character.*

The 'inculcation of religious principles' was, as the Catholic authorities saw it, good reason to treat it with hostility. The parish priest of Lucan, writing to Archbishop Byrne's predecessor, thought it remarkable that while he sometimes had sick calls to Catholic adults in the institution, no sick call was made for the children.

With the passage of time the hostility and suspicion diminished, but Stewart's Hospital remained in Catholic eyes a Protestant institution, and its existence emphasised the absence of an equivalent Catholic service.

The suggestion that the Cabra home should be converted into a special institution for children with a mental handicap was fully

St Vincent's Centre, Navan Road, Dublin, previously the Auxiliary of the South Dublin Union.

The new estate of bungalows at St Vincent's Centre, Navan Road.

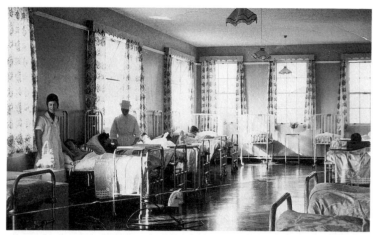

A ward in St Vincent's Centre, Navan Road, Dublin, c.1970.

A bedroom in one of the new bungalows at St Vincent's Centre.

A living-room in one of the new bungalows at St Vincent's Centre.

A house in the Community which is the home of six persons.

'We did it our way'—*Proud winners of medals in the Special Olympics.*

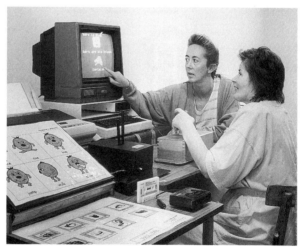

'Keying In'—*Learning through new technology at the Micro Electronics Resource Unit, St Vincent's Centre, Navan Road, Dublin.*

acceptable to the Daughters of Charity, and welcomed by the Commissioners of the Dublin Union, who, like the archbishop, were most anxious for such a service.

The negotiations for the conversion of the home moved quickly. Father John O'Connell, Father Director of the Province, took the leading role in negotiations for the Daughters. Sister Teresa McKenna, who had, at the beginning of 1924, succeeded Sister Martha Galvin as the matron, was also involved in the discussions, and would become the first superior of the new service. After a preliminary round of discussions Father O'Connell informed the Commissioners on 25 August 1925 that the Daughters would undertake the service, and in a further letter some weeks later elaborated the conditions on which the sisters were prepared to operate the institution according to the new concept.

Under the initial temporary agreement arrived at with the Commissioners, the premises at Cabra were leased to the Daughters of Charity for twelve months. The arrangement was subject to the sisters receiving at least two hundred applications for admission before 1 January 1926. It is clear from the correspondence that the sisters had some difficulty in estimating what the costs were likely to be in maintaining an institution filled exclusively with handicapped children. Eventually they agreed to accept £26 annually for each child, up to a maximum of sixty; any children over that number (including children from outside the Dublin area) would be paid for at the rate of £39 per annum by the local authority responsible for the child.

The staff of the home who were then employees of the Commissioners were told that their employment would cease on 31 December 1925. This, in effect, marked the winding up of the old poor law institution. The staff given notice included Sister Teresa McKenna (the matron), fifteen sisters, six lay assistants, and the parish priest of Cabra, Father Warren, who had been chaplain. It is assumed that all of them were absorbed by the new institution, but this is not clear from the records.

With Sister Teresa McKenna as its superior, the new institution came into existence on 1 January 1926 as St Vincent's Home, Cabra.

ST VINCENT'S HOME,
CABRA,
1926–65

The Daughters started their new service with the fifty-four mentally handicapped children already in the care of the home. The large number of other children who had been residents of the former institution were quickly dispersed by the Commissioners: 149 were boarded out, 103 sent to employment, and 176 returned to relatives.

Remarkably, there was not a great rush to secure places in the new home. Although the various local authorities had been made aware of the new service, by the end of 1926 the resident population totalled only 118, mostly children from the Dublin area, with 20 sent by provincial boards of health and 26 admitted on private terms. The prevailing economic climate had given rise to great stringency in public spending and popular resistance to the payment of rates, with the result that impecunious local authorities preferred to continue to use their own county homes — the former workhouses — and mental hospitals when faced with having to provide a place for a mentally handicapped child.

The sisters had always had some doubt about the adequacy of the financial arrangements they had arrived at with the Commissioners. By the end of 1926 their worries were seen to be justified; the less-than-expected use of the home had not helped. When their accounts for the first nine months of the year showed a deficit of over £1,000, the Provincial, Sister Mary Boyle, told the Commissioners that the community was unable to pay the annual rent of £780 that had been agreed upon. The prospect of paying a rent of that dimension was, she said, 'crippling and paralysing'; and she detailed various other unsatisfactory features that had emerged in the operation of the home. There was no central heating; washing installations were antiquated and required renewal; beds needed replacement. No capital funds were available to make any improvements.

Adding to the financial shortages was the fact that parents who had undertaken to meet some of the cost of their children in the home were not contributing. The Provincial complained that, although it was not in the agreement, the sisters were expected to try to collect from the defaulters. Dr Dwyer, one of the Commissioners, could give no consolation on that issue. He wrote in January 1927:

> *It is only by stretching to the utmost limit our powers that we can make any contribution to the cases in question. If, in addition to paying part of the cost of these children's maintenance we had to appoint a collector the cost would be prohibitive.*

The financial problems soured relations between the Daughters and the Commissioners, and they remained difficult over the next year or so. The Commissioners were pressing for the signing of a long-term lease for the home and the twenty acres of land associated with it, but were insistent on the inclusion of a clause that made the lease subject to revision or cancellation after twelve months. The sisters, seeking a greater degree of security, found this unacceptable, and were unhappy with the financial arrangements, including the refusal of the Commissioners to agree to pay the salary of a medical officer appointed by the community themselves. The Commissioners were adamant. They insisted that the sum already being paid to the home was 'distinctly high and compares only with costs in mental hospitals.' Given the dire conditions in the district mental hospitals of the period, the Commissioners were clearly setting a low standard of care for the children in St Vincent's.

With the sisters remaining firm in their refusal to sign the lease on the terms proposed, they were given notice at the end of 1927 that unless they altered their attitude the Commissioners would require free possession of the premises and land on 1 April 1928. Faced with the threat of dispossession, the sisters signed the lease for a term of twenty-one years from 1 July 1928.

A further agreement with the Commissioners on 22 August 1930 spelt out the basis on which they would operate their service. They undertook to accept all mentally deficient and imbecile children sent to them by the Commissioners and 'to support, clothe, maintain, educate and generally care for them . . . ' The Commissioners would pay for each child at the rate of £39 a year. The home would also be free to take in children sent by other local authorities. The sisters agreed to accept as medical officer a doctor in the employment of the Commissioners.

For their part the Commissioners undertook to take children who had reached the age of sixteen from the home when requested to do so by the sisters. From the home's point of view this was an important commitment. The sisters had seen what had happened in Stewart's Hospital, which had long ceased to be an active centre for the training of children with mental handicap as the residents grew into adults and no alternative accommodation was available to enable them to be transferred elsewhere. It was, too, an issue on which a government commission on the relief of the destitute poor had commented strongly when reporting in 1927:

> *No child should be retained in a training establishment at public expense beyond the time when improvement in his/her condition cannot be effected.*

The agreement reached by the sisters and the Commissioners formed the basis on which St Vincent's Home would operate for a considerable period. The number of residents built up quickly from 1928 onwards. Statistics in the annual reports of the Inspectors of Mental Hospitals show the trend:

1928	204
1929	235
1930	255
1931	338
1932	361
1934	411
1935	403
1936	458

In 1936, 194 of the residents were male and 264 female. By now the home had become a national institution: about 60 per cent of the children were from areas outside Dublin. It was also by far the biggest centre for mentally handicapped people in the country: there were then 114 residents in Stewart's Hospital and 59 in St Augustine's, Blackrock, which the Brothers of St John of God had established in 1931 for the care and training of males over school age with a mental handicap.

EARLY DEVELOPMENT OF EXPERTISE

The establishment of St Vincent's Home represented the first public provision of a special service for people with mental handicap in Ireland. Its primary aim was simple: to provide a roof over their heads for children then receiving inadequate care in their families or in institutions not suited to their needs and who in many instances were being neglected. In circumstances where previously there had been no recognition whatever of their special needs, the emphasis was unavoidably on custodial care. While there had always been progressive people, such as Dr Conolly Norman of the Richmond (Grangegorman) Asylum, who had, many years earlier, advocated training and development programmes for people with handicap, there had been little movement in that direction elsewhere and none at all in Ireland. When, then, the Daughters of Charity accepted the task of operating a service, what essentially they had to offer was accommodation, care, and compassion. Yet within two years of the opening of the home an inspector from the Department of Local Government and Public Health reported that improvements in children after a short stay there were 'encouraging and beyond expectation.' Some, unable to walk when admitted, could do so now; some had been taught to speak; others had been trained in habits of cleanliness.

The sisters made no claim to special expertise in advancing the development of the young people placed in their care, and they accepted that they would have to build up the skills to enable them to do that. The subsequent history of the work of the Daughters of Charity for people with a handicap is a striking record of how they succeeded in creating a wide spectrum of expert services — medical, psychological, educational, nursing, and social — all integrated in a scheme of continuous care and treatment.

At first a priority was given to acquiring skills in education. Those working for people with mental handicap were satisfied that they were likely to derive most benefit from services provided when they were of school age. The challenge was to identify the forms and methods of education most suited to their intellectual capacities. Work had been done on this area in Britain, and a number of training courses had been developed for teachers working with handicapped children. From the late 1920s to the late 1950s, sisters from St Vincent's participated in courses held in Manchester, the National Association for Mental Health, London, and Jordanhill College of Education, Glasgow, that enabled them to acquire specialised techniques and curricula and to introduce them into Ireland. Great emphasis was placed on language and story-telling, and the subjects included handiwork, crafts, art, eurhythmics, physical education, and a health programme.

It would be difficult to exaggerate the importance these courses had on the early development of special education in Ireland. Sister Louise Burke, who was appointed principal teacher in St Vincent's in 1944 and later attended a one-year specialised training course in the education of the mentally handicapped in Jordanill College of Education, Glasgow, became a major influence on the direction of special education not only in St Vincent's Home but nationally. Her colleague Sister Gertrude O'Callaghan, another pioneer of special education in Ireland, participated in a similar course under the auspices of the National Association for Mental Health in London in 1947. In addition to the other techniques covered by the courses the two sisters were introduced to the concept of testing and to a range of intelligence and scholastic tests.

Sisters from St Vincent's continued to participate in the courses, which developed in scope over the years. A course in 1953 under the auspices of the National Association for Mental Health for people working in institutions for children with mental handicap covered a wide range of theoretical and practical work. The practical training took place in occupation centres and various hospital departments, and there were 'visits of observation' to nurseries and schools for children within the normal range as well as for those who were mentally deficient.

The participation of the Irish sisters in the British courses was not one-way traffic. It is clear from the records that course sponsors were very pleased with the personal qualities, the commitment and spiritual insights that the sisters brought to the courses. After

Sister Dympna O'Driscoll and a colleague had participated in the London course in 1953 the course tutor wrote to their Superior to say how much they were loved and respected by their fellow-students and how welcome they were wherever they went. Referring to Sister Dympna, who was an 'outstanding student', the tutor, Mrs R. M. Blake, wrote:

> *She has such undoubted ease of manner, coupled with a lively imagination and sense of humour, that children of all ages would be delighted with her classes. Sister Dympna has a natural air of authority and has easily won the respect and affection of her fellow students in particular with her readiness to discuss and explain spiritual matters and the significance of this in the training of mental defectives.*

In February 1947 the Department of Education recognised St Vincent's as a special national school, but no special concessions were given, and the pupil-teacher ratio remained the same as that for ordinary schools. The department had not yet developed a policy on the education of mentally handicapped or 'backward' children, nor were there any formal courses in Ireland that would prepare teachers for this work. Some national-school teachers from Ireland were participating in the five-month course in Glasgow, and the department had started to think about establishing training arrangements in Ireland. The Daughters would play an important part in their development.

FUNDING DIFFICULTIES

The difficulty in getting sufficient funding continued to be a problem in building up the services. Father O'Connell was unsuccessful when, during 1930, he approached Thomas McArdle, Assistant Secretary of the Department of Local Government and Public Health, for finance to establish training in trades. But McArdle encouraged him to embark on a publicity campaign about the work being done in St Vincent's, in the hope that a sympathetic public response would encourage the government to introduce special legislation giving new powers to help the financing of this type of service. There is no indication of the results of the publicity that Father O'Connell subsequently asked the Superior, Sister Rose Brady, to undertake, but in any event it did not lead to new legislation. The financial position of the home remained difficult, and the sisters were forced to borrow £9,000 from their provincial headquarters between October 1930 and February 1932 so that they could continue to operate it.

There was, however, a development at this period that would, in time, make a considerable impact on the growth of institutional services generally for the sick and the handicapped. The proceeds of the Irish Hospitals Sweepstakes, operated by a group of voluntary hospitals, were statutorily taken over in 1931 by the Minister for Local Government and Public Health, and the new provisions gave the Minister power to distribute grants at his discretion to any institution in the health field. In the years immediately before and after the Second World War the Sweepstakes came to be a major source of funding for capital development. While the main priorities were improvements in the general hospitals and the establishment of sanatoriums, the Hospitals Trust Fund, as it was called, provided resources for a considerable extension in services for people with mental handicap, which in the absence of the fund would probably have been far more modest in scale.

St Vincent's Home was authorised to carry out capital improvements during 1935 and 1936 that cost over £25,000, a fairly significant sum at the time. When the sisters proceeded to carry out additional works and sought further funding for them in the region of £10,000, their request gave rise to strained relations with the authorities, which extended over a period of months. The Minister and his department claimed that the work had been done without prior approval. The Hospitals Commission, a statutory body established to advise the Minister on the share-out of the Sweepstake funds, complained about the 'unbusinesslike attitude of the St Vincent's authorities,' and reported to the Minister that the necessity for the work — the provision of a basement — 'was at least debatable.' The Minister paid the £10,000, but with considerable reluctance, and told the sisters that he would not be prepared to give them any further grants from the Hospitals Trust Fund. Furthermore, one of the conditions attached to the grant was that the sisters accept that they could not in future charge any local authority more than fifteen shillings a week for a child maintained in the institution. In addition they were told they would have to furnish the Minister with records of their income and expenditure in a particular form; make the home and its records open to inspection at all reasonable times; and enter into a formal agreement with any local authority wishing to send children to the institution.

While some of these requirements were justifiable, enabling the department to meet its accountability for public funds, the circumstances in which they were sought and the insensitivity shown towards a charitable organisation faced with huge demands on its services represented an extraordinarily harsh, demanding and dictatorial attitude on the part of the Minister and his department.

The legal advisers to the Daughters, writing to McArdle in February 1937, protested at the nature of the charges made and said that the sisters were gravely concerned at the reflections that the report of the Hospitals Commission had cast on the Order. The solicitors also warned that the conditions proposed would have the possible effect of altering the contractual relationship that existed between the two parties. McArdle was reminded that the sisters were merely the tenants of the building they were seeking to improve and that they had been faced with having to accept financial responsibility for some of the work themselves and had had to borrow £13,000, a considerable sum at the time. This had been done 'purely to foster the welfare and interests of the children.'

Father O'Connell, in a letter to McArdle, described in more detail the circumstances in which it had been decided to undertake the disputed adaptation of the basement of the building for the use of some of the children. Many of them were quite helpless and had to be carried up and down the stairs, at risk of injury to themselves. Father O'Connell also kept the Archbishop of Dublin, Dr Byrne, informed about the dispute and complained to him about the 'objectionable and repressive features' of the department's attitude as well as the fact that the Hospitals Commission's report had suppressed some of the facts of the case.

The arguments dragged on for some months, and eventually the issues appear to have been settled after the parties had got together for a discussion. In May 1951 a new lease was agreed with the Minister, which gave the premises to the sisters for ninety-nine years at a yearly rent of £280; but their financial affairs continued to be difficult. Towards the end of 1950, when the sisters sought an increased capitation rate from the Department of Health, Sister Margaret Morris, the Superior of St Vincent's, said that they had an overdraft of almost £20,000, which was 'a bar to all schemes of further improvement.' Over the subsequent years a number of increases were given in the weekly capitation rate, which was adjusted to £1 17s 6d during 1952, and in the same year a further revision of the lease reduced the annual rent to £131 10s. But there was a constant struggle to make ends meet. Sister Ann Maher, who was bursar for a considerable period before lay administrators were introduced, had to struggle valiantly to get by on the parsimonious contribution from public funds. Finally, in 1974, the financing of the services by the Department of Health was based on an annual budget, which went some way towards easing the situation.

DEVELOPMENT AS FEMALE INSTITUTION

The initial concept of St Vincent's Home was that it would be an institution for both boys and girls under the age of sixteen. It was essential to that concept that children reaching the age limit should then be taken back home or transferred to another institution. The original agreement with the Commissioners of the Dublin Union — succeeded by the Dublin Board of Assistance — acknow-ledged the importance of operating on that basis, and the Com-missioners had undertaken to take children reaching the age of sixteen from the home when requested to do so by the sisters. It was easier said than done, and difficulties developed within a few years.

There were problems in finding alternative places. Furthermore, while the sisters were quite happy to care for very young boys, they did not find it easy to cope with the older ones, and had come to the conclusion that they should confine the home to girls. From the beginning they had had a preference for girls, and there was already a preponderance of them in the home's population. The opening of St Augustine's, Blackrock, for young males over school age had been viewed initially as a valuable support to St Vincent's; but the transfers there were few. St Augustine's was a relatively small institution, intended only for 'high-grade' educable males, and in any event it was under considerable pressure for the admission of older boys for whom no previous provision had been made. Furthermore, the population of St Vincent's consisted largely of those with the more severe types of handicap. In 1944, when it had 506 residents, under the classification used at that time the great majority were either 'idiots' (moderately handicapped) or 'imbeciles' (severely handicapped). Few 'feeble-minded' (mildly handicapped) were being admitted.

During 1946 the Archbishop of Dublin, Dr John Charles McQuaid, agreed to a plan of the sisters that in future only girls should be admitted to Cabra. There was then a considerable waiting list of girls, but the sisters were having great difficulty in getting local authorities to take away the older boys from the home to make way for the girls. Local authorities were not happy about young people becoming residents of the county homes, with their mixture of social problems, which was the only option awaiting most of the children who had not got families to take them.

The officials of the Department of Local Government and Public Health had no objection to the conversion of St Vincent's into an institution for girls exclusively, although it is clear from the correspondence that the Dublin Board of Assistance would have preferred the sisters to keep to the original agreement, under which they had undertaken to accept both boys and girls. But St Vincent's moved gradually towards its aim of being an exclusively female institution: at the end of 1949 only 82 of the total population of 469 were male; ten years later, when the total had reached 538, only 49 were male. By then changes in Cabra were being helped by the opening of a number of new institutions for people with mental handicap, some exclusively male.

THE DAILY ROUTINE

During the 1940s and 1950s, restricted financial resources and the absence of a body of specially trained staff meant that the sisters themselves had to carry a heavy burden of work. The children were called each morning at seven; those who could do so made their own beds — in many cases they required assistance. After breakfast the children regarded as ineducable were taken to their appropriate units, where they received care during the day. Those who were educable joined one of two divisions: the first for the higher-grade children, where emphasis was on school subjects, the second for those more likely to benefit from manual work. When classes ended at three there was a period for games or walks. Sister Catherine O'Donnell, a graduate of UCG, taught the boys how to play football. After tea, lay teachers usually came in to teach dancing and craft work.

The sisters themselves were always on duty. The work was demanding, and there was rarely time off. 'All the sisters were committed; you had to be; it would be unfair to pick out anyone as more committed than another,' said Sister Louise Burke. The exhausting work was not helped by the traditional dress that the rules of the order obliged the sisters to wear at all times. The voluminous habit weighed about one stone. The great white head-dress, the 'cornette', had several layers and was 'awful and itchy,' particularly in warm weather. Few of the modern changes in the rules of the Daughters of Charity have been more welcomed than the introduction of their present habit.

Sister Brendan Joyce, who came to St Vincent's in 1948, remembers the hard work and the long hours. 'There were no free days until after Vatican Two.' She recalls the constant shortage of funds: the fact that the Dublin Board of Assistance would often refuse to pay for a child whom the sisters themselves had decided to take because of family circumstances. During Sister Brendan's early years in Navan Road, Sister Rose Brady was the superior. Long after she retired, Sister Rose continued to be interested in the progress of the children individually and liked to be told about them. When Sister Margaret Morris became Superior she insisted on high standards and strict discipline. The limited resources meant that every demand had to be viewed stringently. She would personally distribute the stores and would make sure that there was no extravagance.

Every effort was made to dress the children in the manner of children living outside. Sister Margaret Morris, and Sister Louise Burke, in charge of the school, were determined that those attending the classes should dress like ordinary schoolchildren. The girls wore navy-blue gym frocks, with blouses that varied in colour depending on their division. The boys wore a shirt and tie at school. All changed into more casual wear after school hours. Recalling these years, Sister Catherine O'Donnell said, 'The boys wore short pants for too long — their big knees would be showing.' Later, long trousers were introduced at an earlier age.

The children loved dressing up for their Sunday morning walks — into the Phoenix Park, under the trees on the road leading to the Garda Depot, where they might be lucky enough to see the gardaí on parade; then down to the Liffeyside and home by Aughrim

Street. Sometimes the walk might be across the park to the Furry Glen. In the autumn there was a chance to pick blackberries.

By 1960 or so Sister Rosalie Hurl had introduced the idea of summer holidays for the children who had no-one to take them out. She rented a house in Portmarnock, Co. Dublin, and Sister Gabriel Horgan had responsibility for caring for the groups who were brought there. Many of the then residents recall how hard Sister Gabriel worked to make the holidays a success. There are kind recollections too of how Sister Joseph Rea worked at that period to brighten the daily life of the home, particularly for the boys. She was in charge of the boys' side, and would often bring them out. Chrissie Madden, a resident who assisted Sister Joseph, thought the boys had a better time than the girls because of Sister Joseph's efforts. Sister Joseph took charge of the chopping of the sticks in the winter, when there was no central heating. She also managed to acquire a horse, which the children enjoyed; but the horse was given to straying, and Sister Rosalie Hurl sold him to avoid trouble.

When there was a birthday among the children there was sometimes a cake to celebrate it. A child whose family kept in touch would often get presents; those without close ties outside would get nothing. Bridie Fraughan, a resident of St Vincent's for over fifty years, said, 'I never had a birthday party in my life.' Sister Louise recalls those years. She would like to have made a bit of a fuss about the birthdays of the forgotten children, a small present perhaps, but the sisters individually did not have any money to buy presents with. They became attached to the children in their care, and when the children returned home or passed on to another institution the sisters liked to hear about their later progress. Some of the children were more socially disadvantaged than intellectually handicapped and, benefiting from the care and education they had been given, would later get jobs and marry. Sister Catherine O'Donnell was saddened by the fact that some of the boys, in particular, who grew up in St Vincent's and later went on to have an independent life never came back to see the sisters. It would have meant so much.

Miss Little was one of the paid assistants who came in daily to help with the children. She did this work for many years. Most people do not recall her, but she is remembered with affection

by those who had close contact with her. No-one could recollect her first name: she was simply 'Miss Little' — an indication of the respect she carried with her and her self-effacing manner. She was a small, thin, 'motherly' woman who loved the children and would allow them to remain in bed in the morning when she thought they were unwell. Her judgment was never questioned.

Miss Healion too is remembered with great respect. Her first name was Ursula, but most people called her 'Miss'. This reflected her professional standing and the enormous respect everyone had for her. She was a trained general nurse who came in every day to look after the sick children. St Vincent's was her first nursing appointment after she came out of training. She had chosen it simply because she wanted to work close to her home, which was nearby; she would remain there for forty-five years. Tall, with glasses, she was 'a lovely, gentle, refined woman,' recalls Sister Josephine Flynn. Sister Mary Ryan remembers an outbreak of Hong Kong flu during the 1960s, when about ten of the residents died. Miss Healion 'was marvellous,' and would sit up all night with the sick. She became so much a part of St Vincent's, an embodiment of its ethos of love and charity, that the Daughters affiliated her to the community in recognition of her services, a very special and rarely accorded tribute.

Kit Spring was one of the 'characters' in St Vincent's during the 1960s. She was in her eighties and had been there since the workhouse days. She was fond of Woodbine cigarettes and kept them hidden in her stocking tops. Sister Geraldine Henry was a young schoolgirl then who used to come from Belfast to work for pocket money in St Vincent's during her summer vacations. Kit would send her to buy the Woodbines. Young Geraldine Henry saw in the sisters 'real human beings,' somewhat different from the notions she previously had about people in religious communities. She remembers Sister Clare Hurley in particular and the kind way she had of dealing with the handicapped children. What she saw and learnt about humanity during these school vacations encouraged her to become a member of the Daughters herself. She is now superior of St Vincent's, Lisnagry.

When this account was being written (at the end of 1991) Bridie Fraughan had spent over fifty years in St Vincent's. She came there when she was six, after passing her earlier years in St Philomena's Orphanage, Stillorgan, Dublin. She talks vividly about all aspects of life in St Vincent's, particularly during her childhood. All the traditional institutional features were there. Her clothes were heavy and rough, often passed down from a previous wearer; the underwear was hard and made from calico. All the clothes were made in the home by Mrs Williams and Miss Costello, both of whom were deaf and dumb. There was plenty of food but little variety: porridge and brown bread for breakfast, stew and bread pudding for dinner; big containers and big dishes; long tables with children sitting side by side on benches. Bridie would help with the more disabled children, even when she was still a child herself. By the time she was ten she was sleeping and helping in the infirmary, and would do so for the next forty years.

Her best friend was May Day, older than Bridie and now dead, who worked in the laundry. Like Bridie she had come to St Vincent's when she was a small child and had spent her whole life there. It was said that her name derived from the date on which she had been found as a baby, abandoned and unknown. Bridie too had never known her mother. Thinking about it made her feel sad; she would cry to herself in bed at night and wonder why her mother had forsaken her. Bridie and May would often talk together and try to imagine what the world, about which they knew so little, held for them. If Bridie cried, May would comfort her. May was less emotional. When Bridie was ten she remembers getting sick and being taken to St Kevin's Hospital by ambulance. She spent some time there. No-one ever came to see her; she noticed that other children had visitors.

She has always had a great regard for the sisters in St Vincent's and speaks about them with real affection — even those who were cross with her. 'They had it hard themselves, but they always tried to help you.' Bridie made knitting needles out of two bits of wire and taught herself how to knit. She would unravel old bits of woollen garments to get the wool. Eventually Sister Margaret Morris, 'who kept us on our toes,' bought proper needles for her, and Bridie started knitting for the children. She couldn't read knitting instructions or take measurements, but she would look at the children and always get their size right. Later Sister Mary Ryan would give her pocket money and she would go out shopping occasionally and buy wool and small things that she was putting together for the time when she hoped to have a place of her own. Sister Carmel McArdle showed her how to shop; Sister Marie Barry was 'like a mother' to her; and Sister Bernadette MacMahon was always 'very nice' when she was the Superior.

Bridie remembers Sister Rosalie Hurl for the efforts she made to brighten up life in the home. She organised picnics to Portmarnock. Bridie recalls the excitement of these outings, making sandwiches for the picnic and the journey in the bus. When Dr Lavelle was medical officer to the home he would often give Nurse Healion and herself tickets for the pictures and other shows in thanks for the help they gave him with sick children. She got on well with Nurse Healion, and looked forward to these outings together.

Eventually, Bridie got what she most desired: a place of her own. Sister Carmel helped her to get it, a flat in a house near St Vincent's. Bridie now comes in to work each day in the home and is paid for what she does, just like any other member of the staff. She takes charge of the chapel, and likes serving meals to visitors. She fits easily into the larger world around her and goes with groups to Lourdes and other places abroad. Everyone loves her. To the extent that anyone with a deep sadness in her life can be happy, Bridie is now a happy woman.

POLICIES

DEVELOP;

SERVICES EXPAND

A feature of the years immediately following the Second World War was the increased consciousness of human rights and needs, particularly where disadvantaged and minority groups were concerned. The welfare state evolved. In Ireland, as elsewhere, social issues such as sickness and handicap and their prevention came under closer scrutiny. People with mental illness or a mental handicap became the object of greater public concern than in the past.

The health services in general attracted considerable political attention, which at times boiled over into controversy. The huge problem of tuberculosis was tackled in a more determined way, and special legislation to facilitate the urgent provision of regional sanatoriums came into operation in 1945. During the same year comprehensive legislation was enacted in relation to mental illness. The Department of Local Government and Public Health was divided, and a new Department of Health with its own Minister was established at the beginning of 1947. Later that year the new Minister, Dr James Ryan, introduced a wide range of health provisions, particularly of a preventive nature, in the Health Act, 1947. Proposals by his successor, Dr Noel Browne, for improvements in services for mothers and children led to a considerable political upheaval and the fall of the Government. The succeeding Government implemented the Health Act, 1953, which extended the availability of free and reduced-cost hospital services for people other than those referred to previously as the 'public assistance' class. It marked a significant move away from the deeply rooted principles of the former poor law system still influencing the manner and extent of public provisions for the sick and infirm.

The new social climate was favourable to further expansion in the services for people with mental handicap. The pressure for places in St Vincent's, in particular, was one of the main proofs that there was a great shortage in provision for them. It supported the results of an enquiry conducted by the Hospitals Commission in 1943 that had shown that there was a considerable, and, to a large extent, hidden mental handicap element within the population. Dr Louis Clifford, a psychiatrist on the staff of the Central Mental Hospital, Dundrum, had carried out a survey on behalf of the Commission by examining several thousand children attending schools in selected city and rural areas and extrapolating his findings to the population as a whole. The following extract from the present author's book *Fools and Mad: a History of the Insane in Ireland* (1986) summarises what Clifford's investigation revealed about attitudes towards mental handicap in the 1940s:

> *Sometimes the teachers resented the disturbance of the school routine; many parents were unco-operative; an investigation of this sort was patently unwelcome particularly in rural areas. Clifford's report gives a picture of the taboos and attitudes connected with mental deficiency in Ireland in the early 1940s. Having a mentally handicapped child was widely seen by parents as a disgrace and a reflection on the family. It was especially resented by the higher social strata; those in the lower social groups were more philosophical about their misfortune. Handicapped children were sometimes hidden away in top rooms and seldom taken out except at night. Sometimes those attending school were kept away from it on the day of Clifford's investigation so that they would not be identified as handicapped. This was not a deterrent to Clifford who pursued his work with notable determination. Absentee children were visited in their homes; some fled and were pursued by him through the fields so that they could be brought for examination. At times the investigators found that children in rural schools who prima facie appeared intellectually deficient were backward simply because their*

parents discouraged academic achievements. They feared that a child who did well at school might eventually head for a city career and be a consequent loss to them on the land. Crushed between the academic demands of the school and the hostile attitudes of the parents some children showed signs of emotional disturbance.

Clifford concluded that there were altogether 66,000 people with mental handicap in the country, of whom 21,000 were children. In the light of subsequent and more scientifically devised investigations these figures are now known to be grossly overestimated, and would have included many mildly handicapped people and slow learners who would not today be labelled as handicapped. A census of mental handicap in 1981, for instance, identified 12,304 people who were moderately, severely or profoundly mentally handicapped. It must be emphasised, of course, that Clifford was using different criteria and methods and, as the above quotation shows, had to work under considerable difficulties. In any event, his findings were valuable if for no other reason than because they added to the case for expansion in the existing accommodation provisions.

EXTENSION OF ACCOMMODATION

Some minor additions to the services had taken place before the Government accepted the need for a substantial programme of development. The Brothers of Charity had opened the Home of Our Lady of Good Counsel on the outskirts of Cork for male people with mental handicap, where they purchased a mansion, Lota, and an associated estate in December 1938. Its establishment came before the Government was convinced of the need for developments of this sort, and the Brothers were at first discouraged from extending the accommodation there. They were later given what was described as an ex gratia payment of £2,000 by the Minister for Local Government and Public Health, after strong representations from the local bishop, Dr Coholan. At the end of 1946 they were caring for about eighty residents.

The Brothers of St John of God had by then increased the number under their care in St Augustine's, Blackrock, Co. Dublin, to about two hundred, and had established an auxiliary institution, St Teresa's, Stamullen, Co, Meath, for adult males, where training was given in agricultural pursuits. The Daughters of Charity had themselves, with the encouragement of Archbishop McQuaid, taken the first step of their own towards relieving the pressure on St Vincent's. A small country mansion, the Grange, was purchased at Clonsilla, Co. Dublin, and converted into a centre for adult females. It was named St Joseph's Hospital, and its initial population consisted of forty-three adults transferred there from St Vincent's, Navan Road.

At the end of 1950 there were 1,118 people in the care of special institutions for those with mental handicap, a provision that the Government by now acknowledged fell considerably short of what was required. The constraints previously imposed on new institutional provision requiring public funding were now relaxed, and a substantial programme of development took place during the 1950s. By the end of the decade 2,618 places were available in special institutions, and several hundred other places were in the course of provision. The Brothers of Charity had extended their centre at Lota to 256 places and had opened a new centre at Kilcornan House, Clarinbridge, Co. Galway. The Brothers of St John of God had established St Raphael's, Celbridge, Co. Kildare, with 200 places, and St Mary's, Drumcar, Co. Louth, with 340 places. The Sisters of Charity of Jesus and Mary had opened St Mary's, Delvin, Co. Westmeath, providing 40 places, with a further 240 places in planning. The Sisters of La Sagesse had established Cregg House, Sligo, with 25 places and were planning over 200 other places. Developments at Stewart's Hospital had increased the number of places there to 280. The Cork Polio and General After-Care Association (now 'COPE') had opened a five-day residential school at Montenotte providing for 26 middle-grade mentally handicapped girls and had plans to increase provision to 200 places.

Some of the most substantial developments during this period had taken place under the aegis of the Daughters of Charity. The number of places in St Joseph's, Clonsilla, was increased to 270. In 1950 an offer from the Minister for Health of Glenmaroon, the former residence of Sir Ernest Guinness of the brewery family in Palmerstown, Dublin, was accepted by the sisters and immediately opened as a residential centre, Holy Angels. Following extensive adaptation, a school was opened in 1956, with 235 places. In return for the purchase, equipment and furnishing of the new premises the Minister required the Daughters to give an undertaking to keep not fewer than 500 residents in St Vincent's, Cabra, of whom not fewer than 50 would be children under the age of six. The special school at St Vincent's, recognised by the Department of Education since 1947, was transferred to Glenmaroon.

In 1952 the sisters purchased a country residence and farm at Lisnagry, Co. Limerick, and initially provided 35 places there. Plans to provide an additional 270 places were held up at the end of the 1950s while the Department of Health considered the possibility that the orthopaedic hospital at Croom might become redundant and be handed over to the sisters, thus avoiding a major building programme at Lisnagry. Reacting further to the pressure for accommodation, the sisters decided in 1959 to convert their orphanage for boys at St Teresa's, Blackrock, Co. Dublin, into a residential school for 100 girls with mild handicap, with a further 50 attending on a day basis.

The expansion during the 1950s had been considerably helped by the fact that the Minister for Health was in the advantageous position of having the fairly well-endowed Hospitals Trust Fund at his disposal and was not dependent on exchequer funding for building schemes of this sort. This happy situation did not continue for very long, but it lasted long enough to enable major inroads to be made into a crying social need. Between 1947 and 1960 about £1.5 million in capital grants, a large sum in those times, was given for mental handicap projects. But there was still a long way to go. Despite the new institutions the demand for places was increasing.

Mental handicap within a family was now ceasing to be regarded as shameful, something to be concealed and not publicly acknowledged. Parents and friends of mentally handicapped people were forming themselves into local organisations and demanding better public provisions. At the end of 1961 the National Association for the Mentally Handicapped in Ireland came into existence to co-ordinate the work of the various parent groups and the bodies providing services, and it became a strong collective voice on behalf of the mentally handicapped.

There was increasing resistance to the use of the district mental hospitals for the care of handicapped people. Another important pressure for further provision was a serious problem becoming apparent within the new institutions. None of them had been designed for the accommodation of adults, as it had not been the intention to continue to care for those admitted once they passed the adolescent stage. Yet many children on reaching adulthood had to be retained because of the reluctance of parents to take them back home and the great dearth of suitable institutional accommodation for adults. Furthermore, by 1960 there was serious questioning within the Departments of Health and Education and among professionals in the field whether enough thought had been given to the nature of the problem of mental handicap and to the services required to deal with it in a beneficial and systematic manner.

GOVERNMENT WHITE PAPER

In 1960 the Minister for Health, Seán MacEntee, published on behalf of the Government a White Paper, *The Problem of the Mentally Handicapped*, intended to inform the public about what had been accomplished and to set out the various considerations that arose with regard to the further expansion of the service. The White Paper estimated that when the projects then being planned had been completed, about 3,200 places would be available — a number far short of the 7,000 believed to be required. However, the capital cost of that target would be 'a tremendous burden on the economy,' which would be lightened only by 'success in training patients to become self-supporting and finding jobs for them or by the introduction of a system of domiciliary care.'

It could be said that the White Paper was excessively optimistic about the likelihood of finding open employment for people with mental handicap. It envisaged many of the young handicapped people returning home to their families after a period in training, and finding employment in their own locality. Those who could not return home would live in hostels 'sheltered from bad influences . . . It has happened that these simple souls have been led into mischief and even criminal activities by sophisticated companions of evil tendencies who took advantage of their mental disability.' Those incapable of work would require long-term institutional care. The need for greater emphasis on day services and for better diagnosis and assessment was referred to, but it was accepted that further expansion in the services would come up against the problem of shortage of trained staff and the fact that the religious orders already involved were approaching the limits of what they could do.

54

But over all, the main problem was one of finance. Total public spending on the health services had reached what was then regarded as the enormous sum of £17 million annually, half of which fell on the rates, and it was imperative that the solution to be found 'must, in addition to being effective be as low in cost as it is practicable to make it.' The Minister for Health, a former Minister for Finance, believed strongly that the state should keep tight control on its purse strings and was particularly alarmed about the rapid growth of public expenditure following improvements in health and social welfare provisions. He would have been startled to be told that thirty years later the total annual spending on the health services would have reached £1,500 million, of which about £150 million was being spent on mental handicap alone.

The White Paper was, in effect, the Government thinking aloud: it did not propose any immediate practical measures to ease the problems it referred to. Instead it announced the intention of establishing a commission to examine and report on all aspects of the mental handicap problem. This provoked criticism by opposition parties in the Dáil of what was regarded as the Government's long-fingering of action. A motion moved by Declan Costello TD in November 1960 deplored the Government's attitude, particularly in the light of the great shortage of services for handicapped children. During the ensuing debate the Minister for Health refused to change his stance, and the Commission of Enquiry on Mental Handicap came into existence in February 1961. It reported four years later.

There was nothing radical or unexpected in the commission's recommendations. Its views were based largely on the experience of existing centres in Ireland, Britain, and a number of Continental countries. Its report, for the first time, provided the Government with clear criteria for the organisation and operation of a modern service based on the best current thinking on the subject. While the recommendations would impose clear legal obligations on health authorities to ensure that services were available for people with mental handicap, the commission clearly favoured the provision of these services through the religious orders and voluntary bodies.

The commission's report classified the mentally handicapped into three groups: mildly handicapped (IQ 50 to 70), moderately handicapped (IQ 25 to 50), and severely handicapped (IQ less than 25). In a large number of wide-ranging recommendations it detailed the manner in which the services should be improved. The establishment of expert diagnostic and assessment teams was proposed; education should be provided both for mildly and moderately handicapped children; there should be vocational assessment and placement services in each health authority area; an estimated 900 additional residential places were required for children and about 1,200 for adults; there should be a considerable expansion in day services; the admission of handicapped children to mental hospitals should be discontinued; and the respective roles of the Ministers for Health and Education were defined.

The report now became the guide to the subsequent development of the services.

SPECIAL

EDUCATION

EVOLVES

From the early development of specialised services for people with mental handicap, a distinction was drawn between the provision of education and the provision of care. It was accepted that the education aspects fell within the ambit of the Department of Education, while the caring requirements were seen as the responsibility of the health system. The Commission on Mental Handicap, which had a strong representation of educationalists in its membership, copper-fastened the role of the Department of Education.

During 1939 two school inspectors from the department, Eoin Ó Loinsigh and Bríd Ní Mhurchú, had attended a special course in London in the training of retarded children, and on their return they became the special education advisers within the department. But the war intervened; financial constraints ruled out new services; and it was not until 1949 that recommendations made by the two inspectors started receiving serious departmental consideration. While at this period there was a considerable degree of good will within the Department of Education towards the development of special education, the same could not be said of the Department of Finance, which, devoid of any philosophical stance on the subject other than protecting the public purse, doggedly opposed innovation. When in July 1948 a senior official of that department protested at the possible financial repercussions of the recognition of the special school in St Vincent's, Cabra, she had to be reminded by the Department of Education:

The only repercussions this will have will lie within the [Education] Minister's duties and the State's duty under article 42, sections 3 and 4, of the Constitution to provide for free primary education for educable children residing within the State.

The recognition of the school in St Vincent's came only after unwavering persistence by the sisters. Sister Louise Burke, the principal teacher in St Vincent's, remembers 'endlessly' going to the department to get them to agree, including a meeting with the Minister, Seán Moylan. The school was eventually recognised with effect from 1 February 1947. It was the first residential centre for the mentally handicapped to be recognised as a special school; the first recognised special day school would come considerably later with the recognition of St Michael's School, Northbrook Road, Dublin, in 1960, five years after it had been established.

At the time of the recognition of the school in St Vincent's, 180 of the children there were receiving education from six teachers supported by six assistants. Three inspectors from the Department of Education who had visited the school before its recognition reported that they had 'never seen anything better' and that the school 'was a fine beginning to the education of mental defectives in Ireland.' The inspectors when reporting to their department were clearly disturbed by the parsimonious manner in which St Vincent's was being treated where public funds were concerned. The sisters had to bear, out of their own resources, the costs involved in establishing the school and training the teachers, while the then capitation rate of 17s 4d a week being received for the care of the children from local authorities was 'certainly not enough to feed [the children].'

But the sympathy of the department's inspectors failed to secure any special concessions for St Vincent's from their own department. Recognition as a special school did not bring with it the application of special criteria in regard to staff needs. There was insistence by the department that the pupil-teacher ratio be the same as that for an ordinary national school and that on that basis, four teachers were adequate to deal with up to 185 children in the school.

The four teachers originally recognised by the department were Sister Louise Burke, who had been trained in Carysfort College and

Scotland; Sister Mary Whelan, who had been in Carysfort College and had a BA and HDip as well as having completed a London course; and Sister Enda Brown and Sister Gertrude O'Callaghan, both with Carysfort and London training. The sisters also employed at their own expense a number of well-qualified supernumerary teachers, including Sister Angela Maybery, Sister Agnes Ford, Sister Imelda Galvin, Sister Brenda Walsh, and Sister Vincent O'Donnell. Among the sisters who contributed to the development of the school before it secured recognition were Sister Cecilia Addis, an Englishwoman, and Sister Magdalen O'Sullivan.

In January 1948 the indignant superior of St Vincent's, Sister Margaret Morris, wrote to Seán Moran, the senior departmental inspector responsible for special education:

> *May we respectfully point out that to expect a teacher dealing with mental defectives to handle more than fifteen to twenty children in a class is to render her work fruitless, besides undermining her health. Our own personal experience has been that the mental strain resulting from dealing with this limited number is extremely taxing. Apart from the difficulty arising from the variety of intelligent quotients in any class of twenty mental defectives even more trying on the teacher is the variety of temperaments with which she has to deal. To make personal contact with the children, with a view to understand and so to adjust to them, small groups are essential.*

Departmental papers of the period show that Seán Moran agreed entirely with Sister Margaret's views and regarded it as 'utterly ridiculous' that the staffing rules for ordinary national schools should be applied to special education. Sister Louise Burke recalls Moran's sympathetic interest in St Vincent's and the fact that after he retired he continued to provide helpful guidance to the sisters. It was not until 1956 that the Department of Finance reluctantly permitted the Department of Education to agree to the fixing of the teacher-pupil ratio for special schools at one teacher for twenty pupils. However, irrespective of the department's view, the sisters in St Vincent's always employed the number they regarded as essential, and bore the additional cost themselves.

SPECIAL TRAINING FOR TEACHERS

Special schools required staff with special educational skills. The fact that so few people with this type of training were available was a limiting influence on the expansion of the services. The Daughters of Charity, as the main body concerned, were particularly conscious of the shortage. The opening of Holy Angels, Glenmaroon, in 1955 and the transfer there of the special school from Navan Road, as well as the introduction of day schools in both Glenmaroon and, later, St Teresa's, Blackrock, meant that their existing resources were being spread very thinly.

Other voluntary bodies were faced with similar problems, and the Department of Education was coming around to the view that there was a need to establish a scheme for the special training of teachers in Ireland. As yet there was no clear concept of how such a course should be organised or what its curriculum should be. Sister Margaret Morris, who had been made the first Superior in Holy Angels, was pushing hard for the inauguration of a course, and would have been prepared to consider the possibility of locating it at Glenmaroon. During 1959 the Daughters were asked by the department to run two one-week courses, one in Glenmaroon and one in St Augustine's, Blackrock. The sisters regarded such brief courses as grossly inadequate, but co-operated in their organisation. Sister Louise Burke and a distinguished list of lecturers contributed to them, including Dr Dónal Cregan, president of St Patrick's Training College, Drumcondra; Dr John Stack, Child Guidance Clinic, Orwell Road, Dublin; Dr John McKenna, St Augustine's, Blackrock; and Rev. John McNamara, St Patrick's College.

If the one-week courses fell far short of what was required they had at least the merit of drawing attention to the absence of anything better. Furthermore, the support given to the courses by lecturers and participants had been enthusiastic and an encouragement to future development. There was also the consideration that special education was becoming a political issue. In November 1960 Declan Costello TD had complained in the Dáil about the shortage of special teachers and the fact that there were then only eight special schools in the country.

Father Joseph Sheedy, Spiritual Director to the Daughters of Charity, sounded out Dr Dónal Cregan on the possibility of basing a comprehensive course at St Patrick's College, an approach that was facilitated by the special relationship between the Vincentian Fathers, who managed St Patrick's, and the Daughters. Further discussion followed, in which the college, the Daughters and the Department of Education participated, and it was eventually agreed that the college would establish a postgraduate course for teachers already dealing with children with special educational needs. The first course, in 1961, lasting six months (it was later extended to eight months) was held in Little Denmark Street, Dublin, because of the shortage of accommodation at St Patrick's College. It was the beginning of a form of postgraduate training for primary teachers that would become a permanent feature of St Patrick's, leading to the diploma for teachers of handicapped children.

Sister Louise Burke and her colleague Sister Gertrude O'Callaghan became valued contributors to the course in its early years. Sister Louise had by now become a respected authority on special education and would continue to be seen in that light during her long career as a teacher in the services of the Daughters of Charity. Her important contribution to the shape and content of special education in Ireland is acknowledged by all those familiar with the evolution of the service.

EDUCATION FOR CHILDREN WITH MODERATE HANDICAP

The initial developments in the establishment of special education took place on the basis that only those children in the mild range of handicap were educable. In general there was a pessimistic view about the educational potential of those who were moderately handicapped, although there were some people involved in providing services who always took a more optimistic view. The day school established by St Michael's House in 1955 provided for moderately handicapped children, and was recognised as such somewhat reluctantly by the Department of Education in 1960, as there was a ministerial view that the children were not educable. The sisters in St Vincent's Home had always believed strongly that, with the use of the proper techniques, moderately handicapped children were capable of benefiting from education. The transfer of the special school for mildly handicapped children from St Vincent's to St Michael's, Glenmaroon, in 1956 did not bring to an end the educational programme for the residents with lower IQs remaining in St Vincent's. They were organised into nine groups according to their intellectual ability, and educational programmes were devised for them by a number of sisters who had Montessori qualifications as well as training in Jordanhill College, Glasgow.

When in November 1962 Sister Rosalie Hurl wrote to the Minister for Education asking for official recognition of the classes in St Vincent's, she was informed by the Minister's private secretary that the question of recognition would have to await the report of the Commission on Mental Handicap, then sitting. The commission would not report until 1965, but in July 1963 Sister Rosalie was told by the Department of Education that it would then be prepared to consider the recognition of the school at St Vincent's. 'We knew what the Commission was likely to report and started implementing their findings in advance,' said Mícheál O Mórdha, then one of the senior departmental inspectors dealing with special education. The department's representative on the commission was Tomás Ó Cuilleanáin, Divisional Inspector of National Schools, who would be an important influence on subsequent developments.

The school at St Vincent's for children with moderate handicap was formally recognised in March 1964. Recognition was subject to the condition that only children with an IQ of 35 or more were to be enrolled initially but that after the school had come into operation, the department would be prepared to accept children with a lower IQ when the principal teacher and the inspectors were satisfied that they would benefit from attendance at the school. The department attached great importance to the educational work being done in the school in St Vincent's, viewing it as a pilot project that would assist the department itself in devising policy. When Sister Mary Ryan, the Superior in Navan Road, and Dr John Cooney, medical director, visited the department in July 1964 they were encouraged to apply formally for a grant that would meet most of the cost of a new school building. The new premises were not provided until 1976; by that time there were 120 residential and day pupils undergoing training according to the latest educational techniques for children with a moderate mental handicap.

Special education would remain at a dynamic stage over the 1970s and 1980s as it confronted the challenges presented by the teaching of children with moderate and severe handicaps. The

Daughters of Charity remained active participants in the development of new approaches. Sister Gertrude O'Callaghan, presenting a paper to the World Federation for Mental Health in Dublin in April 1971, urged more emphasis on creative movement and drama to help release the personality of the children. Sister Agnes Forde, principal of the school at St Joseph's, Lisnagry, was a member of a special departmental committee under the chairmanship of Mícheál Ó Mórdha that reviewed the curriculum for the education of the moderately handicapped during the late 1970s and early 1980s. Sister Catherine Tansey, also teaching at Lisnagry, was on one of the subcommittees and later joined the full committee. Sister Catherine remembers the contribution to the committee of special studies made by departmental personnel, notably Seán Mac Gleannáin, Seán Hunt, and Liam Hegarty. The committee issued a series of documents that provided guidance for the schools.

In January 1983 another group, a working party on the education and training of severely and profoundly mentally handicapped children under the chairmanship of Seán Mac Gleannáin, made recommendations that gave a further push to special education. It recommended the removal of any lower limit of eligibility for enrolment in schools for moderately handicapped children; decisions about individual children should be left to the school management in consultation with the inspectorate of the Department of Education. It also recommended that teachers be introduced to residential centres for severely and profoundly handicapped children. This put an end officially to the long-held notion that some categories of children with handicap were ineducable, and it represents a landmark in the progress of the care and understanding of the handicapped child.

FROM
'HOME' TO
'CENTRE'

U nder the influence of new ideas and important developments in Government policy, fundamental changes took place in St Vincent's Home, Cabra, from the mid 1960s onwards.
The recognition of special education and the emergence of a body of specially trained teachers had advanced the quality of the services. The introduction of trained nurses in mental handicap would enhance it further. Much of the care in religious-controlled centres had initially fallen on the shoulders of the members of the communities themselves, but as the numbers of residents grew there was increasing dependence on untrained assistants. In May 1955, following pressure from parent groups, the Department of Health asked An Bord Altranais to consider the need for a special training course for nurses in mental handicap. The board accepted that a course was required, and in 1959 the first training schools for nurses in mental handicap opened at St Joseph's, Clonsilla, and at the centre at Drumcar, Co. Louth, operated by the Brothers of St John of God. St Louise's Training School, as the school at Clonsilla was named, had an original intake of twenty-two students for the new three-year course. A number of other training schools would follow, including one at St Vincent's, Lisnagry.

EMPHASIS ON THE INDIVIDUAL

By the beginning of the 1970s mental handicap was no longer seen as a problem to be dealt with simply by custodial care for large numbers. Such an approach was now history. Caring for people with a mental handicap had come to be based on a more refined concept. The training of the whole person and the aim of 'normalisation' were the main influences on the way the services were being developed and delivered. This approach required emphasis on the individual and a rejection of the notion of caring for people en masse with little or no attention given to the uniqueness of each human being. In furtherance of this approach many of the older residential centres were extensively remodelled, by dividing and partitioning larger rooms, making use of distinctive colour schemes, and generally reducing the harsher and more forbidding aspects of the old buildings.

The emphasis on individuality, on creating a domestic environment, led to the establishment of new centres, such as that at Bawnmore, Limerick, under the auspices of the Brothers of Charity, where a village-style complex of buildings was created. There was a clear shift from custodial care to helping the person with a handicap to remain in the community for as long as possible and in as independent a capacity as possible. This policy was helped by the increasing skills and knowledge of the medical, nursing, paramedical, psychological, educational and other professional groups involved. Within the Departments of Education and Health there was now a body of experts who were working in close association with those providing the services. Dr Bart Ramsay, Assistant Inspector of Mental Hospitals, took a particular interest in mental handicap and is remembered for his commitment to the services and the way he worked to bring about progress. One of his departmental colleagues, senior architectural adviser Justin Tallon, became an authority on the planning of accommodation for people with mental handicap, strengthened by the fact that he had a deep personal commitment to the service. Various official reports and conferences during the 1970s helped to bring a dynamism to the process of change that was under way.

One of the benefits of Ireland's membership of the European Economic Community was that services aimed at helping all categories of handicapped people towards employment became eligible for substantial grants from the European Social Fund. However, Ireland's vocational training services were quite undeveloped and unlikely to meet the criteria that would qualify them for EEC support. A working party drawing on a wide range of expertise was set up by the Minister for Health, Brendan Corish, in January 1974 and, reporting nine months later, set down a broad scheme for the training and employment of handicapped people that secured EEC approval. It led, during the subsequent years, to a considerable flow of funds to Irish statutory and voluntary bodies, including all the main mental handicap organisations, and encouraged the creation of a system of workshops based on the most advanced ideas.

A consultative council on mental handicap established by Erskine Childers when Minister for Health, under the chairmanship of Professor Eva Philbin, reporting in 1975 recommended that greater emphasis be given to day care centres for ineducable children and for adults not suitable for special workshops. It also urged a considerable expansion of pre-school services and more home help support for families of handicapped people. Sister Mary Ryan, then attached to St Teresa's, Blackrock, was a member of that consultative council, as was Dr John Coohill.

ADVENT OF HEALTH BOARD SYSTEM

An important change in the national administration of the health services took place when the health board system came into operation in April 1971. Responsibility for the local provision of health services passed from the local authorities to eight health boards, each responsible for a group of counties. It soon became apparent that there were considerable discrepancies between health board areas with regard to the availability of services for people with mental handicap. This was aggravated by the fact that almost all the residential services were operated by voluntary bodies directly funded by the Department of Health, leaving the new health boards with little power or influence in respect of their own needs.

In the early part of 1975 a series of conferences took place involving the Department of Health, the voluntary bodies and the health boards that led to a number of important decisions setting broad future policy with regard to an equitable organisation of the services on a national basis. It was agreed that these should be regionalised — that most institutions would serve defined regions but some might provide a specific service for a broader area. All applications for admission to residential centres would be channelled through the health boards. People with mental handicap should not in future be referred to psychiatric hospitals. Such people already in those hospitals for a considerable time would remain, but their accommodation would be upgraded, and separate units would be provided for them. Every health board would establish an advisory committee on mental handicap to help the statutory and voluntary bodies to act in unison.

The development of the services remained under continuing review. In September 1979 a working party of the Department of Health, under the chairmanship of Shaun Trant, reporting on progress to date gave its views on the number of further places required in residential centres. It found that there were 6,330 people who needed care in a residential setting, and that this number approximated to the number of places already in existence. However, some of the people then in residential care should have been in the community, and vice versa. Furthermore, some of those in residential care were in the unsuitable settings of psychiatric, geriatric and paediatric hospitals.

Like other recent reports, the recommendations were strongly community-oriented. They urged the provision of more hostels and day services, the assessment of those in residential care with a view to returning some of them to the community, and the review of selection procedures for admission to residential care. The report suggested that the further 1,500 residential places then being planned were sufficient to meet immediate needs, and advised that it would be prudent to await further development of policy before planning additional accommodation.

CONTINUING EXPANSION OF SERVICES

By the end of the 1970s all the earlier services for people with a mental handicap had been expanded or improved in some way. Additional bodies, both religious and lay, were participating in the services. The Sisters of Charity of Jesus and Mary had converted their centre for people with epilepsy at Moore Abbey, Monasterevin, into a largely female centre for people with a mental handicap, and had expanded their services at St Mary's, Delvin, Co. Westmeath. The Rosminian Fathers had opened a centre for male adults at St Patrick's, Upton, Co. Cork. The Brothers of St John of God had added to their existing services a large residential centre for male and female adults and children at St Raphael's, Celbridge, and established largely day services at Islandbridge Centre, Dublin, and Dunmore House, Glenageary, Co. Dublin.

The Irish Sisters of Charity had a large provision of day and residential services for children and young adults at St Patrick's, Kilkenny, and were in an advanced stage of developing a large complex of residential and day services for children and adults with a severe or profound handicap at John Paul II Centre, Ballybane, Galway. The Sisters of the Sacred Hearts of Jesus and Mary had transformed the former home for unmarried mothers and their children at Sean Ross Abbey, Roscrea, into a large residential centre and special school for male and female children and adults. St Mary of the Angels, Beaufort, Killarney, a residential and day centre for males and females of varying ages and degrees of handicap, had opened under the aegis of the Franciscan Missionaries of the Divine Motherhood. The Brothers of Charity had added to their existing provision a wide range of services in the Galway area, notably Kilcornan Training Centre, with both residential and day facilities: Woodlands Centre, Renmore, in which they based diagnostic, assessment and advisory services for the western region, and the large Holy Family School at Renmore, intended mainly for children with a mild degree of learning difficulty. A large complex of services, both residential and day, had been established for male and female adults at Bawnmore, Limerick. The brothers had also developed a residential centre for male adults at Ferrybank, Waterford. Also in Co. Waterford the Bon Sauveur Sisters had transformed a former private psychiatric hospital at Carriglea, Dungarvan, into a residential centre for adult women with moderate, severe and profound handicaps, and had associated with it a large modern workshop where training was given to both male and female trainees.

There had also been a considerable expansion in the range and nature of services operated by lay organisations. Stewart's Hospital was in process of replacing its nineteenth-century accommodation with new units and increasing its community-based services. The former Peamount Sanatorium had been converted into a residential centre for male and female adults with mental handicap. The Children's Sunshine Home, Leopardstown, Co. Dublin, had become a residential centre for young children with various degrees of handicap. Cheeverstown House, formerly a home for convalescing children, had been converted into a large modern complex of residential and day services for children and adults with different degrees of handicap. St Michael's House was rapidly expanding its day services throughout Dublin city and county. Sunbeam House had established a school, training centre and hostel in Bray and was planning other community-based services throughout Co. Wicklow.

The Cork Polio and General After-Care Association (now 'COPE') was expanding its special schools, day care centres, hostels and vocational training services throughout the Cork area. A notable addition to its services took the form of Help Industries, a large EEC-supported training centre at Togher. In Co. Mayo the Western Care Association had established a small residential home, St John's, at Kiltimagh for male and female people with severe and profound degrees of handicap, which had associated with it a rural training unit for people with mild and moderate handicaps. The association had also embarked on a policy of establishing group homes and day services throughout the county. In Duffcarrig, near Gorey, Co. Wexford, and at Ballytobin, Callan, Co. Kilkenny, the Camphill Community had established two village communities where people with a mental handicap and those helping them shared their lives. Based on the same broad philosophical approach, the L'Arche Community had established a small residential centre in Kilmoganny, Co. Kilkenny.

In all areas, organised groups of parents and friends of people with mental handicap were involved in operating community-based services, particularly special schools and day care centres. Notable among these were the KARE organisation in Co. Kildare; Kerry Parents and Friends of the Mentally Handicapped; Galway County Association for Mentally Handicapped Children; Cherry Group Workshop, Ballyfermot, Dublin; Charleville and District Mentally Handicapped Children's Association; the Mother of Fair Love School in Kilkenny; County Longford Association for the Mentally Handicapped, based in St Christopher's, Longford; the North-West Parents and Friends of the Mentally Handicapped, operating the large Rosses Workshop in Sligo; and various other services. In Co. Wexford large community workshops had been organised by parent groups in Enniscorthy and New Ross. In addition the Rehabilitation Institute was in the process of creating a national network of training workshops where people with physical or mental disabilities were being trained for open employment.

While mental handicap services continued to be based mainly on religious and lay voluntary organisations, health boards had found it necessary in some instances to supplement the work of the voluntary organisations. The North-Western Health Board had established a large residential centre in a former religious novitiate at Cloonamahon, Co. Sligo, with the primary aim of facilitating the transfer of people with a mental handicap from St Columba's Psychiatric Hospital, Sligo. The Midland Health Board had converted a former home for unmarried mothers and their children at Castlepollard into St Peter's Centre, again with the initial aim of transferring people with a mental handicap from St Loman's Psychiatric Hospital, Mullingar.

In Co. Dublin the Eastern Health Board was undertaking a considerable programme of building and improvement at St Ita's Psychiatric Hospital, Portrane, to improve the extremely poor conditions of residents with a mental handicap and to create a separate service for them, which is now known as St Joseph's Mental Handicap Service. A plan of the health board to develop a new centre adjoining St Colmcille's General Hospital at Loughlinstown, Co. Dublin, had been dropped, but the board had taken over a former novitiate at Rathfarnham and converted it into the Good Counsel Centre, a residential unit for males and females. In Co. Mayo the Western Health Board was planning a large residential centre at Swinford in association with the Western Care Association. St Raphael's Hospital, Youghal, had continued to develop under the aegis of the Southern Health Board as a residential centre with associated day services for male and female people within a certain range of mental handicap.

The quality of the service given in the various centres during this period was being considerably advanced by the expertise of the developing multidisciplinary teams. People from a range of professions were making their specialised contributions in a systematic, co-ordinated manner to the programmes of assessment, care, and development. Expansion in medical personnel was accompanied by increased numbers of psychologists, social workers, nurses, child care workers, teachers (including Montessori teachers), physiotherapists, speech therapists, and occupational therapists.

As greater emphasis was placed on vocational training, people with training skills from different trades and business occupations were brought in to manage the workshops and devise and implement courses of training.

All in all the extent of the development of the mental handicap services between the late 1960s and early 1980s was remarkable. Their quality and range, and particularly the availability of trained personnel, could stand comparison with the best services elsewhere.

Dr John Cooney's first association with the Daughters of Charity was when he attended St Joseph's, Clonsilla, in the 1950s as visiting physician. He later succeeded Dr Dick Lavelle as medical officer of St Vincent's and Glenmaroon in the late 1950s. He had at the time a large general practice in the Castleknock area, but his involvement with people with a mental handicap stimulated his interest in the problems of mental handicap and the broader area of psychological medicine. In 1961, encouraged by Sister Rosalie Hurl and Dr Jack Fitzgerald, he accepted the post of deputy medical director of the Daughters' mental handicap services. Dr Fitzgerald was the director at that time, the first holder of the post, having previously taken early retirement as resident medical superintendent of St Loman's Mental Hospital, Mullingar. Interestingly, Dr Fitzgerald's father had participated in the work of the royal commission of 1908 on the care and control of the feeble-minded.

Dr Cooney became medical director in 1963 after Dr Fitzgerald had taken the unusual initiative of stepping down and becoming assistant to Dr Cooney. By then Dr Cooney had become a consultant psychiatrist, was a member of the Royal College of Psychiatry, and was pursuing twin specialisations: mental handicap and alcoholism. In this latter role he worked at St Patrick's Psychiatric Hospital, Dublin, where he became part-time associate medical director after foregoing the opportunity to become director of St Patrick's and clinical professor of psychiatry at Trinity College, Dublin. This choice would have obliged him to leave his post at St Vincent's, which he retained until he retired from it in 1985.

Dr Cooney has achieved international status as an expert in alcoholism; it is not relevant to this account to go into the details of his distinguished career in that field. His contribution to the mental handicap area has also been widely acknowledged. He was one of the first chairmen of the National Association of the Mentally Handicapped of Ireland; first chairman of the Federation of Voluntary Bodies in Mental Handicap in Ireland; and Irish representative for many years on the International League of Societies for the Mentally Handicapped. He has served on various Government bodies, including An Bord Altranais (as chairman of the mental handicap committee), the National Rehabilitation Board, the board of the Health Education Bureau, the National Health Council, and the Advisory Council on Health Promotion.

As medical director for the Daughters of Charity Dr Cooney had responsibility for co-ordinating the medical and paramedical work of all the centres. He had the post of deputy medical director established, in which Dr Vincent Molony, Dr Nigel Bark and Dr John Griffin served in succession. Faced with a situation where general hospitals were reluctant to take people who were mentally handicapped, he set about strengthening the medical services in the centres themselves. Paddy McAuley, consultant orthopaedic surgeon, took on a regular visiting role without remuneration. Dr Gerald O'Reilly was appointed consultant ophthalmologist.

John Cooney also believed in the importance of each centre having a strong support group of parents and friends. He instigated the groups at Clonsilla and Glenmaroon, and revived the dormant group at Navan Road. During the critical period of the development of the services in the 1960s to 1980s he became the voice of the mental handicap services of the Daughters of Charity, representing their views and their needs at conferences, in committees, and in negotiations with Government departments. Those who dealt with him found in his diplomacy, balanced views and quiet determination a most effective advocate for the Daughters. To the Daughters themselves he was not only an advocate but also a father figure of considerable wisdom and insight. According to Sister Marie Barry, for a period Superior at Navan Road, 'whenever there was a crisis, Dr Cooney took over.' It is a good summing up of his importance within the organisation.

In 1982, John Cooney had the Papal honour of Knight Commander of Gregory the Great conferred on him by Bishop Dermot O'Mahony at St Joseph's, Clonsilla, in recognition of his services to persons with mental illness and mental handicap.

'Danger—Man at Play'—*In the Community Child Development Centre, Priory Park, Limerick.*

'A Step to Independence'—*Physiotherapy at St Vincent's Centre, Navan Road, Dublin.*

*'**Making a Meal of It**'— Young trainees in the Catering and Accommodation Services Programme at Glen College, Glenmaroon, Co. Dublin.*

*'**A Time for Growth**'—Trainees in the Horticultural Programme at Glen College, Glenmaroon, Co. Dublin.*

'Labour of Love'—*Tofa Craft workers in de Paul Enterprises, Coolmine Business Park, Co. Dublin.*

'Leading the Way'—*Graduates of the first Nurse Training Programme, St Louise Nurse Training School, Clonsilla, Co. Dublin, 1962.* **Back row (left to right):** *Sheila McCormick; Julia Quinlan; Mary Rooney; Mary Feerey; Irene Houlihan.* **Front row (left to right):** *Mary Kiely; Maureen McNamara; Patricia Travers; Elizabeth McLoughlin; Brona McHugh; Sister Josephine Flynn, DC.*

'Young at Heart'—*Katie Mulcaire, oldest resident of St Joseph's Centre, Clonsilla, Co. Dublin with Margaret Meehan.*

From 'Home' to 'Centre'

The service based at St Vincent's continued to change and expand in keeping with new ideas about mental handicap. A challenge to be overcome was the reduction in the numbers in the home: there were far too many residents for safety, or comfort, or the application of more active programmes of care. To help ease the problem additional places were provided at St Joseph's, Clonsilla, to allow the transfer there of some moderately and severely handicapped people. In keeping with the aim of reducing the traditional institutional features of St Vincent's, many rooms were divided, ceilings lowered and partitions erected both in the living and the training areas. The emphasis was on creating small units, on brightness, on distinctive colour schemes.

Speech therapy and physiotherapy services were expanded. The Licensed Vintners' Association made a substantial contribution to the development of the latter department, which acquired a special therapeutic pool within the de Paul Swimming Pool opened in 1971. The swimming pool itself had been financed by a grant from the Department of Local Government and a major contribution from the Friends of St Vincent's, with the Department of Health making up a small shortfall. The pool created an important link with the community when it was opened to public use. In February 1974 the Department of Health agreed to meet the full cost of a social training centre, and the Friends of St Vincent's undertook to finance a new gymnasium, both of which were completed. During this period the Friends had a dynamic chairman in the person of Christy Cooney, who in various ways would continue to be a generous benefactor of the services.

Developments in vocational training services and more optimistic expectations of what they could achieve in relation to people with a mental handicap were a feature of the 1970s. Occupational therapy was already a well-established element of the services at St Vincent's. It was seen by many, however, as not leading anywhere in particular for people with a mental handicap, and largely viewed as a device for keeping people occupied during the day. However, the sisters took a more optimistic view of its potential, seeing it as an important first step in a training process that could lead on to independence. Sister Martha Hegarty, in charge of the unit, was enthusiastic about the possibilities and was sent to London in 1969 to undergo training as a professional occupational therapist. In her absence Gretta Dudley took charge of the unit; Gretta was 'marvellous at bringing on the girls; she always listened to them and had great insight.'

After Sister Martha's return in 1973 a new vocational training unit was planned. Designed by Kidney, Burke, Kennedy and Associates and built by the contractor Christy Cooney, whose commitment to St Vincent's was more than a business one, it was formally opened by the Minister for Health, Brendan Corish, in June 1977. By now funds were available from the European Social Fund to assist services aimed at preparing people with a handicap for open employment, and the new unit was recognised as meeting the necessary criteria. Over twenty teachers and assistants financed by the Departments of Education and Health, as well as by the European Social Fund, provided a wide range of social and occupational training for people under the age of twenty-five regarded as having the capacity for development. Sister Ita O'Leary took a particular interest in developing skills in handcrafts. Most of the trainees were in residential care in St Vincent's; some came in daily from Holy Angels; a number were living in the community.

At one stage thought was given to opening a public shopping arcade in the grounds to provide work for some of the trainees in such skills as home baking, dry-cleaning, and shoe repairs. It would also serve to bring the public into the grounds and help towards the greater understanding of mental handicap. An arcade of small shops was built but was used for other purposes when doubts arose whether it would be successful. In 1985 Sister Martha went to the United States, where she acquired the degree of master of rehabilitation from Michigan State University. She is now responsible for the community living programme, referred to later.

The opening of the Child Study Centre was a particularly important addition to St Vincent's services. Completed in 1974, it became the headquarters of the assessment team composed of psychiatrists, psychologists, and social workers. The team was given a regional role with responsibility for all assessments in north-western areas of the city and for Counties Dublin, Meath, Westmeath, and Longford.

The services at St Vincent's were now expanding along multi-disciplinary lines. Sister Marie Barry and Sister Louise Steen were the first social workers. In more recent times Mary Prendeville held the post of senior social worker as well as taking a prominent role in the affairs of the National Association for the Mentally Handicapped in Ireland. The present incumbent is Anna Jennings. The first senior psychologist was Sister Paul Moriarty, who subsequently transferred to the English Province and was succeeded by Dympna Walsh. Sister Dympna O'Driscoll became the first speech therapist in the service; she had earlier been a social worker. Sandra Allen served as physiotherapist on the staff at a time when the role of physiotherapist in the mental handicap area was still developing.

AN OVERALL PLAN

As the various needs emerged and the process of change accelerated, the importance of an overall plan became apparent. In February 1973 the Sister Provincial, Catherine Barrett, wrote to the Secretary of the Department of Health, Paddy Murray, who took a sympathetic interest in the mental handicap services, outlining the Daughters' concept of the future St Vincent's. It set in motion a planning process that would evolve considerably over the years and is still in the course of implementation. In a formal sense it began the disengagement of St Vincent's from its deeply rooted institutional origins and marked the beginning of the modern mental handicap service now operated by the Daughters of Charity.

In her letter the Provincial made it clear that the sisters wished to develop a plan based on a concept of comprehensive care in which there would be considerable emphasis on community provisions. Apart from any other considerations there was an urgent need for the plan because of 'the recent and somewhat alarming deterioration of the fabric of St Vincent's.' She put forward proposals for an overall scheme. The first phase of implementation envisaged improvements in the main building and the reduction of the number of residents to 350 girls, of whom 100 would be schoolgoing with a high-moderate handicap and the remainder would have a low-moderate or severe handicap. This phase also had provision for a new single-storey building to enable severely handicapped bed cases to be cared for at ground floor level; a sheltered workshop; a unit for day-care patients; a small provision for disturbed residents; a cafeteria; an assembly hall; and a new convent. To a considerable extent these provisions were intended to be of a transitional nature. The second phase would be to remove the vestiges of St Vincent's workhouse origins: the main building would be replaced entirely by a new complex of small units in keeping with modern thinking.

Consideration of the plans moved slowly. By this time capital resources in the Department of Health were again very limited; the Hospitals Trust Fund had become history, and available resources were committed to a wide range of new health projects. A project team to work out the plan in more detail was established under the chairmanship of Dr Cooney and included Sister Marie Barry, the Superior of St Vincent's, and representatives of the Department of Health and the Eastern Health Board. When it reported in November 1978 it had not departed significantly from the proposals outlined above. The 350 residential places for girls would consist of provision for 200 adults and 150 children from the age of four upwards, and it was also envisaged that there would be a substantial number of boys and girls attending on a day basis.

The new complex of buildings, embracing such specialised units as physiotherapy and occupational therapy as well as living units, was designed to serve the needs of different degrees of handicap. The living units would be small, in keeping with the principle of 'normalisation', a concept that had by now become a considerable influence on all developments for people with mental handicap. The plan also envisaged group homes and hostels within the community to complement the services at the main centre, although this type of movement into the community did not get the emphasis that it would receive later.

Consideration of the overall plan did not hold up the implementation of some of its less complex and less expensive elements. Early in 1975 a detached house on Navan Road, quite close to St Vincent's, was acquired and converted into a hostel for eight of the older residents with moderate handicap. The girls went out daily to local employment and acquired a considerable degree of independence. Supervision was minimal. This new hostel represented an important landmark in the new philosophy of care, and provided encouragement for further initiatives of this sort.

From 'Home' to 'Centre'

Now that the service had moved inexorably into a time of change there was a need, from the Daughters' point of view, to make a clear statement of the philosophy and principles that should guide future developments. This statement was contained in *Policy Document: Service for Mentally Handicapped Persons*, published in 1984. It expressed the Daughters' determination to implement all worthwhile new approaches, subject to the realisation and total acceptance of the essential dignity of every human being and his or her sacred and inviolable rights. It stressed that while the services of the Daughters reflected the teachings and values of the Catholic Church, people with mental handicap of other denominations would be cared for and their religious beliefs and practices respected. It reiterated the main aims of the services, particularly the development of the whole person, minimum intervention in family life, maximum integration in the wider community, the placing of emphasis on the quality of life and human dignity, the involvement of parents and other people, the maintenance of high professional standards among staff members, and the adoption of an efficient management structure. It announced the establishment of a Board of Management, which would be responsible to the Provincial Council of the Daughters of Charity for the implementation, development and continuing evaluation of policy.

In January 1987 the new board, in the process of planning for the future, requested two members of the service, Sister Martha Hegarty and Owen Keenan of the social work department, to take a close look at the existing services in the light of current ideas and public policy. They were asked to identify the most appropriate future role for these services and to recommend the changes required in the short and the long term. Their report, prepared in consultation with other senior personnel and with amendments by the Board of Management and Provincial Council, was completed in January 1988 and became the basis of subsequent development.

The report in effect gave expression to the by now considerable experience of the Daughters and their professional advisers and detailed their views about future progress. It reiterated the values and beliefs of the Vincentian philosophy and particularly the recognition of every handicapped person as an individual human being. Its primary recommendations emphasised the importance of an overall policy. All the Daughters' services in the Dublin area should be integrated into a unified service. Those based in Lisnagry should be developed as a mid-western regional service. Once again great importance was attributed to pushing ahead with community provisions, especially community residential projects.

CHANGES PROCEED

The report, its acceptance and the subsequent more detailed planning documents arising from it clarified and accelerated the process of change at St Vincent's. It would now have a much lesser role as a residential centre than earlier thinking had envisaged. The process was considerably hastened following the serving of a statutory fire notice on the Sisters at St Vincent's during 1988 because of fire hazards that had arisen in the old buildings. It was accepted that the existing accommodation there would have to be phased out, with some of its residents transferred to houses in the community, others accommodated in the centres in Clonsilla, Glenmaroon, Blackrock, and Portmarnock, and some returned to their county of origin. St Vincent's in its new role would become the main centre for day activity programmes, and St Joseph's, Clonsilla, would now be developed as the main residential facility for the Dublin service.

By the end of 1991 the services based on or associated with St Vincent's had evolved into a network of residential and community provisions that were a far cry from the basic and exclusively custodial care of the past. The wide spectrum of provisions aims to provide what is sometimes referred to as a 'cradle to the grave' service, one where the child coming into their care is guaranteed the appropriate service for the rest of his or her life, a comforting assurance where families are concerned.

The services at St Vincent's are administered by Sister Rita Yore, while the community living programme is under the direction of Sister Martha Hegarty. The resident population in the centre has been reduced to ninety-five people in six units, four catering for adults and two for both children and adults. The principal concentration is on accommodating people from Community Care Area 6 of the Eastern Health Board, but some people continue to be admitted from elsewhere. One of the significant features of the population is the high level of dependency: three of the adult units cater for people with a severe or profound mental handicap who may also have other serious disabling conditions, including challenging behaviour and mobility problems. All the residents have appropriate developmental and supportive programmes devised to meet their individual needs. Assessment and counselling services are provided through a multidisciplinary team involving medical, psychological, social work and nursing staff. Referrals for assessment, day services and residential places are received from various sources, including parents. A specially constituted committee deals with all admissions to the Daughters of Charity services in the Eastern Health Board area and ensures appropriate follow-up action, including early services for children and counselling for parents. Early services are provided by specialised developmental programmes at St Vincent's and by a small pre-school centre within the community. The programmes are based mainly on the individualised developmental needs of each child.

St Vincent's Special National School caters for those with a moderate mental handicap. At the end of 1991 there were 84 children in attendance, including 15 residing in St Vincent's. In addition 24 children with severe and profound handicap were being educated through a special programme. The teaching staff consisted of a principal and eleven other teachers.

EMPHASIS ON THE COMMUNITY

In accordance with the overall plan the great emphasis since 1988 has been on rooting the services firmly in the community. During 1988–90 twenty-four community-based houses were established, catering for 128 residents. The programme serves mainly people with a moderate mental handicap. The majority of residents in these houses attend the appropriate service daily in St Vincent's and are also supported by the community care services of the health board. Since the houses vary in size and function, the occupancy and staffing levels also vary. Twelve of the houses have five or six occupants with a staff of three; some of the houses with a similar occupancy have a smaller staff; a few houses with residents of high dependency have a somewhat higher staff ratio.

In September 1989 a pilot project based on the L'Arche concept of care began with the establishment of Teach Féile. Under this concept the carers and the cared live together and share their daily lives. Eight people, including three Daughters of Charity, are involved in the pilot project, which is seen by the Daughters as an experimental initiative of considerable importance and in keeping with the basic Vincentian ideal of total commitment to those requiring care and understanding.

The move into the community has increased the role and the responsibilities of the Daughters' social work personnel. All parts of the services work in close association with social workers, who are the primary contact with the family and have an important role in assessing its needs and highlighting its problems. Social workers are particularly concerned in holiday schemes, social and leisure pursuits, and the provision of respite care, mainly through 'Breakaway', an inter-agency project in operation since 1981 that is based on host families within the community.

A feature of recent decades has been the recognition that many people with a serious physical or mental handicap, previously regarded as unemployable, can be vocationally trained and enabled to live an independent working life. This account has already referred to the European Social Fund and to the boost it gave to Irish vocational training services. People with a mental handicap have gained considerably from the services and from the more optimistic view now taken of their potential for employment. Those with a mild mental handicap requiring training receive it within the ordinary educational system and national training agencies. For those with a moderate mental handicap, skill-based training aimed at personal and vocational development has been devised to assist in the transition from school to working life. The Vocational Training Centre at St Vincent's, an important element in the whole structure of services there, provides that type of training for over seventy people, the majority of whom came through the special schools of the Daughters of Charity. As a general rule trainees participate in a three-year programme, although some may complete training at an earlier point or go directly into employment or to a higher level of training elsewhere. The service qualifies for valuable support from the European Social Fund.

Unfortunately, not all trainees find outside employment, either because they have not got the potential or because the general level of unemployment is such that they have difficulty in finding a job. The adult centre that was located at St Vincent's catered for about sixty-five people, most of whom came through the Vocational Training Centre. In October 1991 it moved from St Vincent's to a new centre in Coolmine Business Park. Renamed De Paul Enterprises, it provides a range of sheltered work activity, including light industrial assembly, craft work, knitwear manufacture, embroidery, and packaging.

The comprehensive library that has been developed at St Vincent's is an important resource not only for the various professionals in the Daughters' own services but for others who may wish to consult its wide range of books and journals. The librarian is Sister Bernard McIvor.

Volunteers and well-wishers take an important part in supporting, enhancing and giving firm community roots to the services in St Vincent's. The Friends of St Vincent's, the first such support group in the country, have maintained a continuous fund-raising role for many years and have provided considerable sums for major additions, including the swimming pool, gymnasium, Bowden Hall (named after Joseph Bowden, the Dublin furniture manufacturer who founded the Friends), and St Rosalie's, Portmarnock. In recent times they have raised valuable resources for a new coach and for expensive equipment required for relaxation programmes for residents with a profound handicap. One of the strengths of the Friends has been the long-term commitment of such founding members as the Hogan and Kidney families, and of Dan Delaney and Captain P. J. MacDonagh.

Volunteers from the neighbourhood visit St Vincent's regularly to assist people with a mental handicap using the swimming pool. Other volunteers, largely young people, operate a more long-term 'friendship scheme' in which they befriend particular residents by visiting them and taking them to their homes from time to time or bringing them on outings. The personal benefactions of Christy Cooney, already referred to, have included holiday accommodation at Blainroe, Co. Wicklow.

Sister Louise Burke, whose considerable contribution to the development of special teaching in Ireland has already been referred to, now looks after the Special Religious Education (SPRED) programme. She has done a course in catechetics for

the handicapped.'The idea is that you share your faith with the handicapped, but you first have to help them to understand it,' she says. She has organised small groups of people from the local community to meet small groups of the residents. There is great emphasis on welcoming the visitor, on placing a chair beside each visitor for the friend, on choosing what to do — a bit of artistic work or a jigsaw, perhaps, or handling flowers or leaves, feeling and seeing together the beauty of nature, God's creation. There is a spiritual element in the special relationship, a manifestation of divine love. Sister Louise can sense the appreciation of the handicapped people, even those who cannot speak and may seem completely remote from the world around them.

Sister Catherine Tansey is doing similar work at St Teresa's, Blackrock, and St Vincent's, Lisnagry. Like Sister Louise, she has a long life of working with people with mental handicap behind her and is highly sensitive to their spiritual needs.

This account of the mental handicap service at Navan Road began by referring to the establishment there as St Vincent's Home. At the end of the period covered by this narrative it is clear that this has become a misnomer. It has ceased to be merely a 'home': it is no longer simply a building where a large number of people are receiving residential care; it has become a centre around which a great range of activity and specialised services has developed, reaching out into the surrounding population, where every person with a mental handicap is receiving what is appropriate to his or her needs. It now faces the future as St Vincent's Centre — another and perhaps the final stage in its evolution from Cabra Auxiliary Workhouse, and a remarkable transformation in the services that the first Superior and her small community established there one hundred years ago.

ST JOSEPH'S,

CLONSILLA

St Joseph's, Clonsilla, was established in 1943 following the acquisition of the Grange, a small country mansion. The initial population of forty-three residents were adults transferred from the severely overcrowded St Vincent's, Navan Road. During the subsequent years the house was remodelled and considerable additional accommodation provided in a new single-storey structure laid out in separate units. Later three specially designed group homes, each accommodating ten girls, were added. An occupational therapy unit for a hundred trainees was opened in 1964 by Mrs Seán Flanagan, wife of the then Minister for Health who had provided a generous grant to supplement the contribution of the Friends of St Joseph's.

By the mid-1970s the total resident population was in the region of three hundred. Sister Rosalie Hurl was the first Superior, and her successors during the formative years of the centre were Sisters Monica Carlin, Monica Gallery, Paul Ronayne, and Catherine Galvin. Sister Catherine went on to serve as Superior in Holy Angels, Glenmaroon.

Sister Patricia Lynch, the present Superior, began working in St Joseph's about 1960 but was absent for some years while she was doing her general nursing training. She recalls having to care for a unit of thirty-five residents with the aid of a single assistant aged thirteen. Things are far better now: there are more staff, and the residents are in smaller groups, but there is a greater level of dependency among the residents since the more active members have moved out into the community. Some of those in residence are now in their seventies and eighties. Looking back over the years, Sister Patricia recalls in particular Sister Ita McCullough, who 'did an awful lot.' She remembers, too, the devoted work of Sister Frances Duffy.

Sister Brendan Joyce came from Navan Road to St Joseph's in 1956. She and others recall with admiration Nurse McCann, who served on the staff from 1958 to 1982. She was Nurse 'Cann' to the residents: a great personality who always made visitors feel welcome when they came to see their relatives. Sister Brendan also remembers 'great characters' among the residents, particularly Josie Tracey, who did most of the sewing and clothes-making. She was also a great story-teller, with a wanderlust and an urge for adventure in the outside world. Sometimes she would rove away and cause considerable alarm, but would always turn up safe. Once she hid in a basket of laundry being sent to Glenmaroon, because she was curious about Glenmaroon, a place she had never seen.

With many years of working for people with a mental handicap behind her, Sister Brendan has always been struck by their forgiving attitude. They never maintain grudges: if they have a row they make it up. 'It's the one great thing I learnt from them,' she says.

When the training school for nurses in mental handicap, St Louise's, opened at St Joseph's in 1959, Sister Bernard Coey was in charge of the first three-year course of training. Sister Josephine Flynn, now Superior at St Teresa's, Blackrock, was the only Daughter of Charity on that course: all the rest were lay students. By comparison with the current curriculum for the course, the initial one was thorough but relatively simple.'There wasn't any talk about holistic medicine,' says Sister Josephine. The school is now the national applications centre for all people wishing to train in mental handicap nursing, but the selection process is carried out by the individual nursing schools. Dr Jack Fitzgerald, the first medical director of the service, took a special interest in the nursing school from its inception. Many of its graduates still recall his lectures and his interest in their careers.

At the end of 1991 St Joseph's was the largest residential centre operated by the Daughters of Charity, providing for about 250 women between the ages of twenty-five and eighty-five. The majority were over forty-five; many were frail and required intensive medical and nursing care. In addition a number were exhibiting challenging behaviour, and special programmes were being provided for them.

The main building had been organised into eight large units, and five group homes were also in use. Sister Patricia is particularly grateful for the way the outside community has helped the home over the years and made life more interesting for the women living there. A very active Friends' Association met the cost of a new assembly hall and purchased and extended a house in Malahide as a holiday home. A Ladies' Committee takes residents on outings regularly, brings them to visit their own families and takes them back again, and remembers the birthdays of those who would otherwise have no-one to give them presents. A Friendship Scheme involves volunteers forming friendships with particular residents. There is also a social club for the residents, where there is tea and chat and music. The first patron of the Friends' Association was Lady Honor Svejdar, and its first chairman was Philip O'Donoghue SC.

Annie O'Toole has spent about sixty years as a resident in Navan Road and Clonsilla. She was six when she originally came to St Vincent's, and was in the first group to be transferred to St Joseph's. A life in the open air had always attracted her, and she loved St Joseph's from the beginning, particularly before the old house was extended and when there were plenty of trees and green spaces. The sisters kept five cows, a pig, three hundred hens, thirteen turkeys, and eleven ducks. Annie remembers the numbers because she fed them all.

The neighbours next door had horses and let Annie and the other girls ride them. She tells funny stories about runaways and clutching their tails for safety. All the animals and poultry have gone now, and Annie misses them, but the garden compensates. She loves all its seasons; the flowers and the vegetables; planting and sowing and taking cuttings. She likes the sun but doesn't mind the rain or the wind; her tanned and weather-beaten face reflects her life. She works closely with the gardener and has a small detached hut where, of her own choice, she takes her meals. She has no friends or relatives outside, and her eyes fill with tears when she talks about the way life cut her adrift from the ordinary world. The pleasures of the garden and

the kindness of Sister Patricia make up for much, but there is an underlying sadness. The old, dignified Annie O'Toole with her sense of humour and her love of the natural world around her is a reproach to the perceptions and attitudes that set apart the child Annie O'Toole so many years ago.

9

HOLY ANGELS,

GLENMAROON

Holy Angels has always had an important supporting role where St Vincent's, Navan Road, was concerned, and this has been facilitated by the fact that the two centres are quite close to each other, on opposite sides of the Phoenix Park.

The buildings and the surroundings in Glenmaroon are of considerable beauty. The house actually consists of two separate buildings: the North House, a three-storey building in the Edwardian Tudor manor-house style built for Ernest Guinness in 1905, and the South House, the original building, Knockmaroon Lodge, built around 1838 as a two-storey Victorian country house, to which additions were made later. The houses are separated by a public road but until recently had been linked by a corridor bridge, which had to be demolished for safety reasons. A new linking bridge was opened in November 1991.

On entering the buildings through the main entrance of the North House one steps into a spacious foyer with beautifully carved oaken woodwork, including a striking staircase and an ornate stucco ceiling. On one side of the hall there is a study with an Adam fireplace; on the other side, a large music room with panelled walls and stucco decorations. The original furniture in the house had been sold before the sisters took up occupation there. When the Superior, Sister Margaret Morris, set about refurnishing it, she was pleased to find in a Dublin showroom a number of items that fitted easily into the setting of Glenmaroon; without knowing it she was in fact purchasing some of the original furniture of the house! The buildings are in a beautiful setting overlooking the Liffey valley, with terraced lawns and planted areas reaching down to the river. Two tall redwood trees dominate the wide variety of trees and shrubs in the grounds.

Sister Margaret Morris was the first Superior in Holy Angels. By now she had become one of the key figures in the development of the Daughters' services. She had acquired a tremendous amount of experience during her twelve years in charge of Navan Road, and was seen by her superiors as having the acumen, drive and vision necessary to get new services organised and operational. Later she would be involved in the planning of St Joseph's, Clonsilla, and then go on to be the main architect of the services at Lisnagry. She was succeeded as Superior at Holy Angels by Sister Catherine Galvin.

Sister Gertrude O'Callaghan, who had been teaching in the school in Navan Road, recalls the move to Glenmaroon in April 1955. The pupils and the sisters involved were transferred there by bus, 'tadpoles and all' (some of the children had collected tadpoles on their regular walks in the Phoenix Park and did not wish to be parted from them). For a time there was no furniture in the accommodation allocated to the school, and since the weather during the first few months there happened to be good the teachers found it more pleasant to teach the children out of doors, under the lush hedges in the grounds.

The new school premises opened in 1956 under Sister Louise Burke. Sister Gertrude became principal in 1959, and remained in the post until she ceased teaching in 1980. She has kind words to say about the Department of Education officials with whom she dealt; from the earlier years she recalls Bríd Ní Mhurchú, Seán Moran, Tomás Ó Cuilleanáin, Mícheál Ó Mórdha, and Mr Frewen, who helped the school get a more favourable teacher-pupil ratio. She remembers too how some of the department officials would help to transport the children to their summer holiday home.

Sister Finbar Nagle also went to Glenmaroon with the original group from St Vincent's, where she had been for most of the time since 1943. She recalls the impact made on the girls by the grounds and the non-institutional aspects of the house, so different from the nineteenth-century workhouse environment to which they had been accustomed. She remembers the excitement at the new sights, the unaccustomed freedom of the grounds and buildings. The goldfish pond was a place of wonderment. Sister Finbar pays tribute in particular to the work done in the school in these early years by Mrs Beda Brophy, who was vice-principal and 'a marvellous teacher.'

Recent Superiors in Glenmaroon who contributed significantly to its development were Sister Francis O'Leary and Sister Patricia McLaughlin. Both had served as principal of the special school at Navan Road before their appointment to Holy Angels.

By the 1970s the school had 160 boarders and 60 day girls and was operating as much as possible as an ordinary school, with practically all the pupils returning home for the normal school holidays. There were fifteen whole-time teachers under a headmistress, complemented by specialists in psychiatry, psychology, speech therapy, physical education, dancing, drama, and music. One of the earliest psychologists in Glenmaroon was Dr Anne McKenna, who worked there on a part-time basis.

The school curriculum placed considerable emphasis on social and vocational training and development. Music became an important part of the programme. Sister Gertrude and Annie Griffin, one of the lay teachers with an interest in music, combined very successfully to bring out the talents of the girls. Annie had musical connections (Carl Hardebeck, the composer, was a relative). She was the main inspiration behind the establishment of a harmonica band, which won prizes on several occasions in the Dublin Feis Cheoil. The school also had a prize-winning percussion band. There were always great festivities in the school when the children returned from the feis with a cup. It was like the homecoming of an All-Ireland football team!

An old building adjacent to the school, formerly used as stables, was developed into flats, creating a domestic setting in which the girls were taught how to organise their daily lives in as independent a manner as possible before passing out into the community. A job placement service was established, involving a number of social workers based at Holy Angels working in close association with the placement services operated by the National Rehabilitation Board.

In 1974 a large house was purchased on the North Circular Road with the help of a grant from the Department of Health and converted into a hostel for ten school-leavers. It remains in use and has been an important bridge between the school and an independent life; over the years many girls have lived there while they found their feet outside. The Friends of Glenmaroon, an association of relatives, friends, and well-wishers, have been very active in helping the progress of the girls towards independence, particularly in their financial support for the flats and the hostel. The late Lord Iveagh, a grandnephew of Sir Ernest Guinness, the former owner of Glenmaroon, was patron of the Friends. The first chairman of the association was Dr Harry Counihan.

Subsequent to the 1970s there were important changes in the nature of the population in Glenmaroon. From a peak of 200 school boarders the number had fallen to about 20 at the end of 1991. While there is a continuing high level of demand for special education at the school, the great majority of the children on the rolls — almost 200 at the time of writing — attend on a day basis. The situation reflects the general move away from residential care and the increased family support services.

The ordinary school curriculum is followed but is adapted to meet the individual needs of the pupils. Teaching is at a functional level, so that it is relevant to the life skill needs of the children. The subjects include English, mathematics, history, geography, art, language development, social skills, environmental studies, computer-assisted learning, pottery, woodwork, horticulture, and leisure pursuits.

As part of an integrated response to problems that some of the school-leavers may have in moving from school into independent adulthood, a small hostel has been established in the grounds, where advice, guidance and counselling are given to those seeking it.

During 1990 a vocational training programme was established at Holy Angels to provide for the continuation training of school-leavers in particular skills, leading to recognised qualifications. This training facility has been named Glen College. The college is in the charge of Mark Sheehy, who was formerly a placement officer with the National Rehabilitation Board and has had over twenty years' experience in the horticulture industry, and he has a number of trained horticulturists on his staff. The courses include trainees sponsored by FÁS. The principal courses are in horticulture, commercial catering and household services, office skills, and general crafts. It is a particularly appropriate setting for horticulture training. In the days of its former glory as a Guinness estate cared for by a big staff of gardeners, the grounds had a large formal garden, now sadly overgrown; the horticultural college may provide an opportunity to tackle its restoration. While the primary aim of the college is to provide training, it will also produce fruit and vegetables for the catering departments of the Daughters' services and for sale on the open market.

The reduced number of boarders in Holy Angels has freed accommodation for a service for adult people with a moderate to profound handicap and has helped to take some of the pressure off St Vincent's, Navan Road. The division of the buildings at Holy Angels by a public roadway has facilitated the separation of the educational activities from the adult service on the northern side of the road. The latter service includes residential and respite care and associated day activation, personal development, and recreational activities. The residential accommodation is provided in the North and South Houses and in the former flats — now renamed Ozanam Villa — where the majority of residents have individual rooms and live in a homely atmosphere. Sister Angela Magee is responsible for the overall administration of the services at Holy Angels as well as being the mission co-ordinator for the Mental Handicap Services of the Daughters.

Eileen (not her real name) was one of the first residents in Glenmaroon. As a baby she was abandoned by her mother in a church and taken to the shelter of St Patrick's Home, an institution for unmarried mothers and their children. At the age of three-and-a-half she was brought to St Vincent's, and at nine she was transferred to Glenmaroon, where she spent the rest of her child-hood. She is now a happily married woman who travels daily to work in Glenmaroon.

'Why was I regarded as a handicapped child?' she asks. It is hard now to find an answer for her and to justify the fact that her childhood had to be spent outside normal society. As in the case of many other children who formerly grew up in institutions, the answer lies in the insensitive attitudes of the past towards children born outside marriage, rather than in Eileen herself. But she has no grievance where the sisters are concerned: they 'had hearts of gold.' Sister Margaret Morris was 'a mother', who had no favourites because all the children were important to her.

Eileen loved all the music in the school in Glenmaroon. She was in the choir; Sister Gertrude O'Callaghan trained them and taught them to sing an office in Latin. Eileen was also a member of the prize-winning harmonica band. She was not particularly fond of the ballet classes, but she loved the ballroom dancing: the tangos, the foxtrots and the quicksteps and the popular tunes of the period played on records in the classes given by Mr and Mrs Janette. She is happy now. Light-heartedly singing the words from 'Amazing Grace', she says: 'I was lost but found.'

ST VINCENT'S,

LISNAGRY

S t Vincent's, Lisnagry, Co. Limerick, differs from the other mental handicap units of the Daughters of Charity in that it serves a different region of the country and is not part of the interrelated services that have evolved for the Dublin area, largely influenced by the needs of the parent centre in Navan Road. It is not, nevertheless, entirely independent of the Daughters' services in Dublin. It is an important element in the overall plan for their mental handicap services, and its present and future roles are subject to the philosophy and concepts of that plan.

When, in 1952, the Daughters acquired Lisnagry, a country residence and farm previously owned by the Goodbody family on the eastern side of Limerick city, there were as yet no special services for persons with a mental handicap in the Limerick area. It remained until the 1960s a small residential centre for about thirty children, all girls. The first Daughters to take up residence there were Sisters Columba Kennedy, Kevin Shannon, and Kevin Dullea. Sister Columba Kennedy, the first Superior, was a kind, 'motherly' woman who loved the children, took them on outings, and was determined that the centre should not operate in the traditional institutional manner.

During the 1960s a comprehensive building programme took place, financed mainly by grants from the Department of Health. It created a large complex of units with a range of facilities for moderately and severely handicapped children. As yet there was no emphasis on creating small family-type units: the general aim was to create an atmosphere remote from that of the traditional large institution and to establish a centre where there was emphasis on light, on colour, on space, and on hygiene. Much of the dynamism for innovation came from the Superior at this time, Sister Margaret Morris, whose contribution to the development of other centres we have already seen. Sister Catherine Tansey, who came to Lisnagry in 1964, remembers Sister Margaret as very determined and far-seeing, with a 'powerful presence' but very warmhearted and kind. Sister Geraldine Henry, now Superior in Lisnagry, remembers being 'in awe' of Sister Margaret when she first met her.

Jack Darby, who was then the principal officer in the Department of Health with responsibility for policy in the mental handicap area, recalls how businesslike and efficient Sister Margaret was in developing the service. She died in September 1971.

Sister Mary Gardiner was another Superior who served in Lisnagry for a period during its developing years. Before coming there she had been matron of Gateacre Grange, a private nursing home in Liverpool, and had also been matron of St Vincent's Psychiatric Hospital, Fairview, Dublin.

The original intention was that St Vincent's should be a residential centre for girls, but day services for both boys and girls were gradually developed, and a small number of boys admitted to residential care. By the mid-1970s there were 200 children in residence, a majority of them attending the special school at the centre, and in addition about 40 children were attending the school on a day basis, helped by a school bus service.

Sister Agnes Forde was for a long time the principal in charge of the school. Sister Kevin Shannon, one of the first teachers there, is remembered with particular regard. Sister Catherine Tansey remembers how patient and persistent Sister Kevin was in teaching children with major learning difficulties. In the early days at Lisnagry, before the school was properly established, she would take the children into the fields when the weather was fine and, as they sat around her in the grass, teach them the elements of reading and writing. She had no doubt that more than anything else it would create for them a link with the everyday world. Josie Hughes, who grew up in St Vincent's and now works there, recalls with gratitude how Sister Kevin taught her to write. Sister Kevin continued to teach in Lisnagry for almost thirty years, until she retired in the 1980s.

There was a degree of inevitability about the changes that gradually took place in the character of the population of St Vincent's. They followed a familiar pattern. While originally planned to provide exclusively for children who, it was expected, would transfer to another service on reaching adulthood, it was found that this was not possible in practice. There had been an expectation with the opening by the Brothers of Charity of the large village-type complex of services for male and female adults in neighbouring Bawnmore that adults in residential care in St Vincent's would be transferred there. However, such was the demand for the new services, particularly from people previously unprovided for, that the possibility of relief for Lisnagry was ruled out.

In the meantime the complex of facilities at the centre continued to develop. A new physiotherapy unit was opened; the special school was extended; a modern chapel was opened. In more recent times a gymnasium was added; the units were refurbished; a hydrotherapy pool costing about £400,000 was in the course of building at the time of writing. The Lisnagry Parents' and Friends' Association have been the major fund-raisers of some of these projects. In addition, the J. P. McManus Pro-Am Golf Classic donated £170,000 towards the pool. The residents of the local parish of Castleconnell also take an interest in the centre and organise a Christmas party every year for the children.

In 1970 Dr Jim Ledwith was appointed medical director of the service at Lisnagry. He had previously been attached to St Patrick's Psychiatric Hospital, Dublin, and had been encouraged by Dr John Cooney to join the Lisnagry service. Later he also accepted the post of medical director of the Brothers of Charity service at Bawnmore, as well as becoming consultant child psychiatrist to the service operated by the Sisters of the Sacred Hearts of Jesus and Mary at Sean Ross Abbey, Roscrea. His involvement in the three centres has contributed to an important degree to the co-ordination of the services for people with a mental handicap in the mid-western area.

In 1973 St Vincent's was recognised by An Bord Altranais as a training school for nurses in mental handicap. A new building was provided for the purpose, and Sister Rita Yore became the first tutor in the school, later serving as Superior between 1983 and 1989. Sister Geraldine Henry, one of the first group of students, took the same path as Sister Rita by becoming tutor in 1988 and succeeding her as Superior in 1989.

At the end of 1991 the pattern of services reflected the movement towards community care evident in other centres for the mentally handicapped. There were 155 residents in the centre, with a further 33 girls accommodated in seven community houses. The residents, over 70 per cent of them adults, ranged in age from one to fifty, representing all categories of handicap. Eighteen of the residents were male. In addition, day services were being provided at St Vincent's for 139 people, male and female, of whom 103 were attending the special national school with about 30 of the residents.

There was a high degree of dependency among those being admitted both to the residential and to the day services. Many had, in addition to their principal handicap, accompanying physical handicap or behavioural problems that required a broad range of medical, rehabilitation, therapeutic and activation programmes. Sister Catherine Tansey, with almost thirty years' experience of teaching in special schools, detects increasing problems in recent times among children attending the school in St Vincent's, probably reflecting the emotional pressures that many children undergo in the modern family setting.

Pre-school services originally provided within St Vincent's are now catered for mainly by the child development service at Priory Park, which was established in 1990 within the city area. At the end of 1991 about thirty children under the age of five were availing of the service. Lisnagry's social work service has strong links with that of the Mid-Western Health Board, thus facilitating the sharing of information and the co-ordinating of services. Great importance is given to relieving families under pressure, and the 'Have a Break' scheme, similar to 'Breakaway' in the Eastern Health Board area, provides holiday breaks for children with handicaps.

The organisation of programmes for the occupational training of people leaving the education system is similar to that at St Vincent's Centre, Navan Road. A Skill Base programme has been developed at Lisnagry, devised to meet the individual needs of participants. A new supported employment unit has recently been opened at the Tait Centre, Limerick, where the Daughters hope to create a small sewing and textile business. On completion of the programme some of the trainees may move on to vocational training under the direction of the Brothers of Charity or may go into supported (sheltered) employment in the Daughters' own service. The programme qualifies for support from the European Social Fund and provides training in a range of skills, including catering and canteen work, woodwork, crafts, printing, horticulture, and garden maintenance.

Josie Hughes grew up as a resident in St Vincent's, Lisnagry, and now leads an independent life, although she continues to work there. She shares the former gate lodge with Kitty, Esther, Mary Teresa, and Rose, all former residents who go out to work daily. Josie found life in St Vincent's as a child often very lonely, particularly when most of the other children went home during holiday periods. She remembers the kindness of Sister Margaret Morris, who gave her a small room for herself after she had slept in a dormitory for many years. She is fond of music; plays the mouth organ; organises the choir; and acts as receptionist for visitors to Lisnagry.

Nancy Quinn, who lives in one of the community houses at Castletroy, also comes to work daily in Lisnagry. She has four companions in the community house. The neighbours never come near them, but Nancy thinks that if she sought help from them it would be given. She travels to London occasionally to see a brother and sister who live there. She is a good cook and does most of the cooking for the Sisters. She speaks well of the way the Sisters treated her when she was growing up in Lisnagry. Sister Kevin Shannon has a special place in her memories, because she meant a lot to Nancy. She taught her what she needed to get on in life, and Nancy has done that.

11

ST TERESA'S,

BLACKROCK

St Teresa's, Blackrock, was originally an orphanage for boys, but in 1959, when there was a lengthy waiting list of children with learning difficulties and mild handicaps, the Daughters changed its use to that of a special school for such children. New, specially planned school accommodation was added in 1962, the old buildings were renovated, and an educational and caring programme similar to that at Holy Angels was developed. A hostel for eight girls was established two miles away at Booterstown, and this became an important support to helping girls towards open employment and independence.

The first Superior of St Teresa's was Sister Gabriel Horgan, and she was followed by Sister Mary Brady and Sister Magdalen Kelly. Sister Catherine Tansey was one of the first members of the staff following its changeover. She recalls all the dull brown paint and the general lack of colour throughout the buildings. She remembers shopping for bright curtains and colourful fittings so that a new and more pleasant atmosphere could be created before the girls arrived.

At its peak during the 1970s there were about 100 pupils in residence in St Teresa's and about 50 attending on a day basis. Under the influence of the new approaches, considerable changes took place subsequently in the nature of the demands on the school. With the move away from residential care and the increasing provision for slow learners within the ordinary education system, the number of residents gradually declined, and the school closed in June 1987. The residential pupils were transferred to Holy Angels, Glenmaroon, and the day pupils to the neighbouring St Augustine's special school for boys and girls operated by the Brothers of St John of God. St Teresa's now became an important support unit to St Vincent's Centre, Navan Road, and helped to reduce the population of that centre during the dispersal that took place in 1988. Forty residents were transferred there from Navan Road, all adults in the moderate to severe range of handicap requiring continuing residential care.

At St Teresa's, residents participate in programmes of activation, training and development in the social development centre, which had been the school in former days. An in-service course for staff themselves, 'Values to Practice', places stress on dignity, relationships, and communications. Great importance is attached to planning individual programmes for each resident, and this is facilitated by the small number of residents in the centre and the fact that they are organised into four separate units. Sister Josephine Flynn, Superior of the centre when this account was being written, had no doubt about the effectiveness of the programmes and the great advantages that a small centre has over the larger traditional institutions.

The personal development of the residents has been notably advanced by a 'friendship scheme', under which local people, largely young people, are encouraged to come into St Teresa's regularly and to form friendships with the residents. They talk to each other, have tea together, listen to music. The volunteers take the residents to their homes, to the pictures, or on other outings, and are given a small financial allowance to help them do so. The scheme is devised especially for those who are never visited by their families; it creates an important new element in their lives, something they never had previously or had long forgotten. 'It gives them a great lift,' says Sister Josephine. 'You notice the excitement, the way they make themselves up when their friends are coming.'

ST ROSALIE'S,

PORTMARNOCK

All those who served with Sister Rosalie Hurl remember her with pride. She has already been mentioned on various occasions throughout this book, and was undoubtedly one of the outstanding figures in the development of the mental handicap services of the Daughters of Charity. After being the first Superior in St Joseph's, Clonsilla, she went on to be Superior in St Vincent's, Navan Road, where, in the prime of life, she died in office, from cancer, in May 1963.

Dr John Cooney had come quickly under her influence when he first started working at Navan Road, and it was with her encouragement that he decided to develop a specialised interested in mental handicap.

All her contemporaries recall her vitality. Sister Brendan Joyce remembers her as 'an outstanding person,' full of ideas and determined to upgrade the services. 'She transformed St Vincent's,' said Dr Cooney, recalling in particular the extent to which she advanced the hygiene of the home by the addition of a modern kitchen and laundry. The recurring problem of dysentery disappeared.

She had a persuasive personality, with the valuable capacity for favourably influencing Government officials. Jack Darby, who dealt with her as a senior Department of Health official, found her to be a most impressive and committed woman. Sister Rosalie was determined that the residents in St Vincent's should not become institution-bound and that they should have greater contact with the world outside. She organised the first group of them to travel to Lourdes in the late 1950s, and was also the first to organise a holiday home especially for those who did not have a family to take them on holidays. She rented a house for that purpose in Portmarnock, and this innovation proved such a success that she offered to buy it from its owner so that it would be available as a permanent holiday home. The owner, Mr McCarthy, required the house for his own family, but generously presented Sister Rosalie with an adjoining site on which a new home was eventually erected. Sadly, Sister Rosalie died before it was completed, but it bears her name; standing on a rise overlooking the magnificent Portmarnock strand, with distant views of Lambay Island and Ireland's Eye, it is an imposing commemoration of her work.

In 1988, when the number of residents in St Vincent's, Navan Road, had to be urgently reduced, it was decided that St Rosalie's should make a contribution by becoming a separate residential centre. At the end of 1991 it was providing accommodation for twenty-four women residents, aged between twenty and forty-three, almost all of whom had a low, moderate or severe level of handicap. There has been considerable support for the home in the surrounding community, where Father Harry Gaynor, a local curate, was very successful in securing the involvement of his parishioners. The local leisure centre has been made available to the residents free of charge twice a week. Neighbours come into the home regularly, make friends with the residents, and take them for walks.

The Superior of the home is Sister Zoe Killeen, who was trained in mental handicap nursing in Clonsilla and later completed general nurse training. She takes an optimistic view of the further social development of those in her care. She is pleased with her staff of sixteen and their interest in new ideas. Reflexology has been introduced, with beneficial results. Sister Zoe sees considerable possibilities in computerised techniques as an aid to learning, and welcomes the intention to develop the micro-electronic research centre at St Vincent's as a national resource for the promotion of microtechnology-assisted learning.

CENTRAL

MANAGEMENT

ORGANISATION

The development of a modern multi-faceted service for the mentally handicapped has brought about fundamental changes in the management of the services of the Daughters of Charity. Even if the number of women joining the Daughters had not declined there would still have been a need to seek outside the community itself some of the special management skills necessary to operate the large, expensive services in an efficient way.

To put the situation in context: at the end of 1991 there were about 1,500 people with mental handicap receiving services from the Daughters. These services were being provided by a staff of about 900, including 36 Daughters and about 50 teachers and assistants employed by the Department of Education. The annual cost of the services is in the region of £14 million.

For a considerable period the services had been managed by the Daughters along traditional lines. Overall control was vested in the Sister Provincial and the Provincial Council of the Daughters. The internal administration of each centre devolved upon the Sister Superior of the centre, who was appointed by the Provincial and the Council, to whom she was responsible. She had responsibility for all aspects of the operation of her institution: finance, appointment of personnel, disciplinary action, building development, and maintenance, as well as the many aspects of the daily operation of the services. While she could call on the support and advice of her superiors and her professional advisers, the sister in charge of a centre clearly carried a considerable burden of responsibility.

Central Management Organisation

In the early 1970s the sisters were joined in the management of the service by Ted McGrath, a professional accountant with a background in the general hospital system and experience in dealing with the financial areas of statutory authorities. It was an important transitional step, for he brought with him a valuable expertise that prepared the way for the later establishment of a new management structure. Ted McGrath retired in 1987. Around this time Sister Carmel McArdle was seconded to St Vincent's as Administrator following the completion of a specialised management course. Sister Carmel made a considerable impact on the service by the introduction of new management techniques, as well as by her industry and commitment.

NEW MANAGEMENT STRUCTURE

Following the review of the future role and shape of the services and the publication of the policy document of 1984, an important change was made in the management structure. The Provincial, Sister Pauline Lawlor, and her Council established a board of management, which now consists of the Provincial, Assistant Provincial, Provincial Councillor of the Mental Handicap Service, the Sister Administrator of each of the centres, the immediate past Provincial Councillor, the immediate past Sister Administrator of Holy Angels, and Dr John Cooney. The new board became responsible for the continuing review of policy, for sanctioning any major developments, and for creating and making appointments to senior posts (other than those involving sisters). It also assumed an important degree of financial control to ensure an equitable distribution of funds among the different centres.

The board is appointed by the Provincial Council of the Daughters, to which it is accountable. The Council has the power to 'disband or change the structure of the Board should it deem this to be in accord with the best interests of the services.' The chairperson of the board will always be a Daughter of Charity.

The management structure was further strengthened following the report on the evaluation of the service in January 1988, which concluded that there was a need for a director of services and supporting senior personnel to implement the policies of the board of management and generally oversee their operation. The composition of the board of management was changed to reflect the new management structure, and now consists of the Provincial as chief executive officer of the service, Assistant Provincial, two other members of the Provincial Council, including the councillor with responsibility for the service for people with a mental handicap, Dr John Cooney, and Kevin O'Donnell.

In May 1989 Joseph Fallon, formerly a senior army officer, took up duty as director of services, and a number of supporting appointments were made, including a mission co-ordinator, financial controller, personnel manager, planning and development officer, and logistics officer.

Dr John Cooney had retired as medical director in 1985 and was succeeded by Dr Jack Halpenny, who retired in February 1991. He was succeeded by Dr Martin McLaughlin, already on the staff of St Vincent's, whose vacancy has been filled recently by Dr Patricia MacCarthy. The medical services have been further strengthened by the employment on a sessional basis of Dr Ann Power, consultant child psychiatrist. The central management team works in association with the service co-ordinating committee, which meets monthly and is responsible for the preparation and submission of proposals to the board of management. The committee consists of the Administrator of each centre and of the community living programme and the central management team.

The development of the new management structure in recent times has been an important innovation. While it recognises the inappropriateness of the traditional organisation of the Daughters for the management of expensive, complex, multi-disciplinary services, it represents no diminution in the influence of the Vincentian philosophy and its role as the core of the service. The Daughters of Charity, while enlisting the skills of lay experts for day-to-day management, retain control of the services and thereby ensure that their traditional values and ethos are firmly preserved.

FUTURE DEVELOPMENT

A detailed plan for the future development of the services has evolved in a series of planning documents prepared by the Provincial Council and management of the Daughters in association with their professional advisers. The rate at which the plan will be implemented will depend on the availability of funds, particularly financing by the Minister for Health. The relationship between the Daughters and the statutory bodies has been marked by co-operation, understanding, and good will, and the Daughters look forward to the continuation of that happy situation. In general the future progress of the services will proceed along the path they have already taken: towards the recognition of the individual needs of all people with a mental handicap, towards enhancing their quality of life and their dignity, with minimal interference, away from large institutions and notions of caring for people en masse.

In Dublin the Daughters of Charity, as a voluntary agency, will continue to plan their services on the basis of providing, in association with the Eastern Health Board, an integrated service for Community Care Area 6. This extends over the northern parts of the city and county, with a population of about 150,000. It is envisaged that early intervention and pre-school services will be strengthened by the establishment of local multi-disciplinary teams. The main development at St Vincent's Centre, Navan Road, will involve the withdrawal of the last residents from the obsolete workhouse building and their transfer to a complex of ten bunga-lows, planned in the style of an ordinary housing scheme, on the adjoining land. Eight of the bungalows will be designed to accommo-date seventy-six people with a severe or profound handicap. There will also be a ten-bed respite unit and a fifteen-bed challenging behaviour unit. The scheme will involve the demolition of the west wing of the old building.

The Minister for Health, Dr Rory O'Hanlon, turned the first sod for the scheme on 23 May 1991, and the new residential accom-modation will become available in 1992. It will not provide places for all the residents at St Vincent's, but it is expected that the additional requirements will be met within the community. Planning is at an advanced stage for the provision of new facilities to replace those located in the obsolete buildings. These facilities will include a day activation centre, resource centre, kitchen and dining complex, and administrative offices.

Other improvements at St Vincent's Centre will include an expansion of the speech therapy services, additional staff in the day activation units for children and adults, a better central library service, improved allowances for residents engaged in household duties, and a strengthening of the vocational and independence training services. An important addition to family support services will be the establishment of three teams of domiciliary care workers to supplement the respite and crisis care services.

A major element in the future concept of St Vincent's will be the relocation outside the centre of the supported employment services so as to create as normal a work setting as possible. This will require two new work units at different ends of the community care area. The first of these units has been occupied at Coolmine Business Park.

It is also proposed to develop the existing micro-electronic research centre as a national resource for the promotion and support of microtechnology-assisted learning for people with a mental handicap. Where research in general is concerned, it is proposed to promote actively investigation and evaluation that will contribute to the body of knowledge available to those providing services. At present an important study is being carried out by Mitchel Fleming aimed at establishing the comparative impacts of care in community and residential settings. The results of research initiatives at the centre are likely to be of wide interest, and it is intended to seek national and international financing for the work.

The other Dublin services all require various degrees of improvement in line with current ideas. The main thrust of future change at St Joseph's Centre, Clonsilla, will be towards reducing the occupancy of large units by creating additional smaller units of accommodation in the centre and by a reduction of the overall numbers there through relocation as well as through death. The aim is to maintain the centre at a capacity of approximately 150 places. A number of improvements in the staff and facilities are envisaged, including the establishment of a hydrotherapy pool.

The services based at Holy Angels, Glenmaroon, will be improved by the purchase of additional houses within the community for those attending the school. A purpose-built recreational activity centre is required for those in residential care, as well as a range of additional staff. The organisation of the residential service at St Teresa's Centre, Blackrock, into six units for groups of from five to eight residents will require staff expansion there also.

At St Rosalie's, Portmarnock, inadequate facilities for the activation and social development programme will be met by minor accommodation extensions and additional staff. The community living programme requires a continuing provision of additional accommodation to maintain the clear community orientation of services. It is planned to provide new individual units within the community, collectively forming a block development and including a warden's unit, which will provide general supervision and support for the complex. It is also intended to acquire a house to provide respite care for people normally living at home who may need respite support from time to time.

Services associated with St Vincent's, Lisnagry, will continue to expand and improve to meet the needs of the Mid-Western Health Board area in association with the health board and the services of the Brothers of Charity at Bawnmore. Among the improvements envisaged are increases in personnel to meet the demand for the early intervention, developmental and pre-school services. The day activation services for adults require a purpose-built area, comprising individual units in which special programmes can be carried on. Additional community houses are essential to maintain movement into the community. There is an urgent need to develop the services for children in the severe and profoundly handi-capped categories who also have serious behavioural problems. Additional resources are also required to meet the needs of the increasing number of people requiring sheltered employment. In general the services associated with Lisnagry need a strengthening in staff numbers to meet the growing demands and increasing specialisation of the services.

CONCLUSION

The Daughters of Charity, their colleagues and advisers have a clear vision of the way in which they wish to see their services progress in the future. Their plans will remain flexible so that they can be adjusted from time to time in the light of new ideas and advances in therapy and training. The progress of recent times justifies an optimistic view, the setting of new and more distant horizons.

As this account has shown, the story of the evolution of our modern services for people with a mental handicap has been marked by radical changes in expectations and achievements, particularly during the last few decades. Social rejection and care of a purely custodial nature gave way to the emergence of special edu-cation and the recognition of its possibilities. This was accompanied by a progressive movement from large institutions where residents were cared for en masse to smaller residential units and day services, to village-type complexes, to family-size houses within the community. This progression was stimulated and accompanied by a growing recognition of the rights, the dignity and the individuality of each person with a handicap and by a far more optimistic view of what they could be helped to achieve. The most recent Government review of the progress of the service, *Needs and Abilities: a Policy for the Intellectually Disabled*, published in July 1990, in effect gives firm official blessing to the type of policies that the Daughters of Charity have been implementing in recent years.

The Daughters have been an important part of the story of the progress of the services in Ireland over the last century. They themselves are unlikely to trumpet what they have achieved. Their humility, and their mission based on Christian love and Vincentian commitment to the less fortunate members of society, would see their achievements as merely doing what they vowed to do. Those outside their community will make their own judgments and will salute the work of a remarkable band of women.

APPENDIX

SISTER VISITATRICES OF THE PROVINCE OF GREAT BRITAIN
AND IRELAND, MILL HILL, LONDON

Sr Minart, 1885–90
Sr Marcellus, 1890–1918
Sr Hannezo, 1919–26
Sr Mary Boyle, 1926–28
Sr Anne Thomson, 1928–46
Sr Gerard Burke, 1946–47
Sr Joseph McGee, 1947–52
Sr Margaret Whalen, 1952–66
Sr Gertrude Andrew, 1966–78

SISTERS PROVINCIAL (PROVINCE OF IRELAND ESTABLISHED
1 SEPTEMBER 1970)

Sr Catherine Barrett, 1970–76
Sr Pauline Lawlor, 1976–86
Sr Bernadette MacMahon, 1986–

FATHER DIRECTORS OF THE PROVINCE

Fr William Gavin CM, 1885–98
Fr Joseph Walsh CM, 1898–1909
Fr William Byrne CM, 1909–22
Fr John O'Connell CM, 1923–38
Fr Joseph Sheehy CM, 1938–61
Fr James Cahalan CM, 1961–67
Fr Felix McAtarsney CM, 1967–80

Appendix

Appendix

St Vincent's, Navan Road, 1892–1992: Sr Martha Galvin, Sr Teresa McKenna, Sr Rose Brady, Sr Louise Duffy, Sr Margaret Morris, Sr Patricia McGouran, Sr Philomena Allen, Sr Clare Ryan, Sr Margaret Morris, Sr Rosalie Hurl, Sr Mary Ryan, Sr Gertrude Mannion, Sr Marie Barry, Sr Bernadette MacMahon, Sr Angela Magee, Sr Clare Hurley, Sr Sheila Ryan.

St Teresa's Blackrock, 1959–92: Sr Gabriel Horgan, Sr Mary Brady, Sr Magdalen Kelly, Sr Gertrude Kelly, Sr Clare Hurley, Sr Gabriel Horgan (second term), Sr Joseph O'Mahony, Sr Agnes McKenna, Sr Mary Ryan, Sr Francis Keogh, Sr Genevieve Prendergast, Sr Anne Killeen, Sr Josephine Flynn.

St Joseph's, Clonsilla, 1943–92: Sr Rosalie Hurl, Sr Monica Carlin, Sr Monica Gallery, Sr Paul Ronayne, Sr Catherine Galvin, Sr Mary Ryan, Sr Marie Barry, Sr Angela Magee, Sr Patricia Lynch.

Holy Angels, Glenmaroon, 1950–92: Sr Margaret Morris, Sr Catherine Galvin, Sr Frances O'Leary, Sr Patricia McLaughlin, Sr Gertrude O'Callaghan, Sr Angela Magee.

St Vincent's Lisnagry, 1952–92: Sr Columba Kennedy, Sr Mary Gardiner, Sr Margaret Morris, Sr Mary Collins, Sr Patricia Lynch, Sr Rita Yore, Sr Geraldine Henry.

St Rosalie's Portmarnock, 1990–92: Sr Zoe Killeen

SOURCES

References to the origins of the Daughters of Charity are drawn from M. V. Woodgate, *Louise de Marillac: the First Sister of Charity*, Dublin 1942.

The account of the beginning of the Cabra Auxiliary is based to a considerable extent on miscellaneous correspondence of the period in the archives of the Daughters of Charity in Dunardagh, Blackrock. The general background in relation to poor law policy and the care of children in workhouses is drawn from Joseph Robins, *The Lost Children: a Study of Charity Children in Ireland, 1700–1900*, Dublin 1980. Information about the North Dublin Union workhouse in the later decades of the nineteenth century comes mainly from the *Report of the Select Committee on Poor Relief (Ireland)*, July 1861, minutes of evidence, House of Commons papers 1861 (408) x; *Report of the Poor Law Union and Lunacy Enquiry Commission (Ireland)*, 1879, (C. 2239), xxxi; *Report of the Reformatories and Industrial School Commissioners*, 1884 (C. 3876), xlv; annual reports of the Local Government Board of Ireland; J. D. H. Widdess, *The Richmond, Whitworth and Hardwicke Hospital: St Laurence's, Dublin, 1772–1972*, Dublin 1972.

Most of the biographical material about Sister Martha Galvin is taken from the archives of the Provincial House of the Daughters of Charity, Mill Hill, London.

The description of life in the children's home during 1892–1926 is based mainly on the minute books of the North Dublin Union (National Archives); reports from inspectors of the Office of National Education (in the archives of the Daughters); *Report of the Viceregal Commission on Poor Law Reform in Ireland, 1906* (Cd 3202), li; Joseph Robins, *The Lost Children*. The account of a public enquiry into the need for a Protestant church in the home is drawn from reports in the *Freeman's Journal and the Irish Times*, 26 April 1902. The reference to William O'Brien is based on Printed Pamphlets, etc., a gift of William O'Brien in the National Library.

Sources

The background to the beginning of a service for people with mental handicap in Ireland is based on the sources already listed, as well as the annual reports of the Inspectors of Lunacy in Ireland; the *Report of the Royal Commission on the Care and Control of the Feeble-Minded* (Cd 4221), xxxiv; minutes of evidence HC 1908 (Cd 4217), xxxvii, xxxviii; minute books, Commissioners of the Dublin Union, 1918–25 (National Archives); miscellaneous papers of Archbishops Walshe and Byrne (Dublin Archdiocesan Archives); *Report of the Royal Commission on the Poor Law and Relief of Distress — Report on Ireland, 1909* (Cd 4630), xxxviii; and Joseph Robins, *Fools and Mad: a History of the Insane in Ireland*, Dublin 1986.

The description of St Vincent's, Navan Road, since 1926, draws on archival records and on interviews with staff and former residents who are identified in the text and in the acknowledgments. The annual reports of the Inspector of Mental Hospitals contain statistical information regarding the home.

The account of the development of special education leans heavily on the unpublished thesis of Éamonn Ó Murchú, 'The Establishment and Development of Special Educational Services for Mentally Handicapped Persons in the Republic of Ireland, with Special Reference to the Period 1955–1965'. Mr Ó Murchú also gave me access to miscellaneous papers on the subject in his possession. Interviews with Sisters Louise Burke, Catherine O'Donnell and Brendan Joyce also provided background information. An interview with Mícheál Ó Mórdha, formerly of the Department of Education, was also valuable. The Government report of January 1983, *The Education and Training of Severely and Profoundly Mentally Handicapped Children*, was another source.

To a large extent the account of developing policies subsequent to the 1950s draws on official publications, notably *The Problem of the Mentally Handicapped* (1960); *Report of Commission of Inquiry on Mental Handicap* (1965); *Dáil Debates*, November 1960; and Department of Health papers A122/106 in the National Archives. The account of services in more recent times and the developing policies of the Daughters of Charity is based on archival records, John Cooney's booklet *A Service for the Mentally Handicapped*, and the various planning and policy documents prepared by the Daughters and their advisers during the period 1984–91. I have also had the benefit of my own recollections of the long period I spent as an official of the Department of Health, when I had some involvement with the mental handicap services.

INDEX

Index

Index

Hospitals Trust Fund, 40, 53
Hughes, Josie, 94, 97
Hurl, Sr Rosalie, 45, 48, 62, 71, 83, 100
Hurley, Sr Clare, 46

industrial schools, 4, 24
Irish Hospitals Sweepstakes, 40
Irish Poor Law Commissioners, 3
Islandbridge Centre, 68
Iveagh, Lord, 90

Jannette, Mr and Mrs, 92
Jennings, Anna, 75
John Paul II Centre, 68
Jordan Hill Training College, 38, 61
Joyce, Sr Brendan, 44, 84, 100

KARE, 69
Keenan, Owen, 77
Kelly, Sr Magdalen, 98
Kennedy, Sr Columba, 92
Kerry Parents and Friends, 69
Kidney, Burke, Kennedy and
    Associates, 74
Kidney family, 81
Kilcornan Training Centre, 52, 68
Killeen, Sr Zoe, 101
Kingstown Children's Home, 22

Lavelle, Dr, 48, 71
Lawlor, Sr Pauline, 103
Ledwith, Dr Jim, 95
library, 81
Licensed Vintners' Association, 73
Little, Miss, 45, 46
Local Government Board for Ireland,
    3, 5, 11, 16, 17
Lynch, Sr Patricia, 83, 85

McArdle, Sr Carmel, 48, 103
McArdle, Thomas, 39, 41
McAuley, Paddy, 72
McCann, Rita, 84
MacCarthy, Dr Patricia, 104
McCarthy family, 101
McCullough, Sr Ita, 84
MacDonagh, Capt. P.J., 81
McDonnell, John, 12, 13
MacEntee, Seán, 54
Mac Gleannáin, Seán, 63
McGrath, Ted, 103

McIvor, Sr Bernard, 81
McKenna, Dr Anne, 89
MacKenna, Dr John, 60
McKenna, Sr Teresa, 33
McLaughlin, Dr Martin, 104
McLaughlin, Sr Patricia, 89
MacMahon, Sr Bernadette, 48
McManus, J.P., 95
McNamara, Rev. John, 60
McQuaid, Archbishop J.C., 43
Madden, Chrissie, 45
Magee, Sr Angela, 91
Maher, Sr Ann, 42
management of services, xi, 76, 102–8
Marcellus, Sr, 9, 12
Maybery, Sr Angela, 59
meals, 18–19
mental handicap
    in asylums (mental hospitals) 27,
        28, 53, 57
    Commission of Enquiry, 28, 29, 30,
        31
    consultative council, 66
    development programme, 51–3
    early provisions, 26
    organisation of services, 66, 67
    special education, 57–63
    White Paper 1960, 54, 55
    in workhouses, 27, 28
    survey of, 50–51
    government review 1990, 108
micro-electronic research centre, 106
Midland Health Board, 70
Mid-Western Health Board, 96, 107
Minister for Education, 56, 58, 62
Minister for Health, 53, 54, 55, 56
Minister for Local Government and
        Public Health, 40
Molony, Dr Vincent, 72
Moore Abbey, 67
Moran, Seán, 59, 88
Moriarty, Sr Paul, 75
Morris, Sr Margaret, 41, 44, 47, 59, 87,
        88, 94, 97
Mother of Fair Love School, 69
Moylan, Seán, 58
multi-disciplinary teams, 70
Murray, Paddy, 75

Naas Workhouse, 29
Nagle, Sr Finbar, 88

Index

Index